Berlitz®
Crete

Original Text: Lindsay Bennett
Updater: Paul Hellander
Text Editor: Jeffery Pike
Managing Editor: Tony Halliday

Berlitz® POCKET GUIDE

Crete

Ninth Edition 2004

PHOTOGRAPHY
Berlitz 41, 59, 108; Donna Dailey 8, 23, 33, 51, 53, 68, 70, 72, 78, 93, 110; Glyn Genin 6, 9, 10, 11, 13, 15, 16, 17, 18, 20, 25, 28, 35, 37, 38, 39, 42, 45, 46, 47, 48, 52, 55, 57, 61, 64, 66, 73, 76, 80, 81, 83, 84, 90, 97, 100, 102, 103, 105, 109; Topham Picturepoint 24, 26; Gregory Wrona 29, 31, 54, 62–3, 75, 86, 88, 95, 99, 104, 107
Cover: Peter Adams/Taxi/Getty Images

CONTACTING THE EDITORS
Every effort has been made to provide accurate information in this publication, but changes are inevitable. The publisher cannot be responsible for any resulting loss, inconvenience or injury. We would appreciate it if readers would call our attention to any errors or outdated information by contacting Berlitz Publishing, PO Box 7910, London SE1 1WE, England.
Fax: (44) 20 7403 0290;
e-mail: berlitz@apaguide.co.uk
www.berlitzpublishing.com

➤ The prettiest town in eastern Crete, Ágios Nikólaos (page 53) is a popular resort that preserves its Cretan charm

◄ The Samariá Gorge (page 82) – the longest in Europe – is a strenuous but exhilarating trek

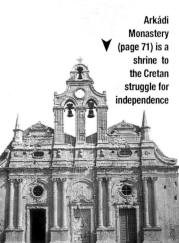

Arkádi Monastery (page 71) is a ▼ shrine to the Cretan struggle for independence

TOP TEN ATTRACTIONS

Ancient Gortys (page 44) was the capital of Crete in Roman and Byzantine times

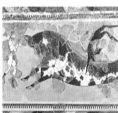

The Minoan palace (page 39) at Knossos, with its superb frescoes, is Crete's most-visited attraction

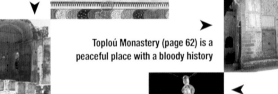

Toploú Monastery (page 62) is a peaceful place with a bloody history

Iráklio's Archaeological Museum (page 34) is packed with priceless Minoan finds

Rural life and ancient windmills on the Lasíthi Plain (page 58)

Venetian and Ottoman buildings crowd round the lovely harbour at Haniá (page 77)

The mighty Fortezza in Réthymno (page 68) is the largest fortress ever built by the Venetians

CONTENTS

A ➤ in the text denotes a highly recommended sight

Fact Sheets

INTRODUCTION

Crete: the name invokes a range of different images. Ancient sites to explore; commercial towns bustling with noise and traffic; millions of olive trees blanketing the countryside; raucous resorts with neon-lit bars and loud music; a romantic meal for two overlooking small fishing boats in the harbour; mountains to climb; a sun-bed on a beach among thousands of others similarly soaking up the rays; 15 hours of sunshine a day in summer; three feet of snow in the mountains in winter. This island has a little something for everyone, and its sheer variety satisfies even the most jaded and cynical traveller.

The 'Great Island'

Crete sits in the eastern Mediterranean Sea, just 200km (125 miles) north of the African coast and a short journey by boat from Israel. Its strategic position at the crossroads of trade north from Egypt, west from Rome and east from Mesopotamia and Arabia made it a valuable piece of land from the earliest days of trade and political power brokering.

With its area of 8,300 sq km (3,200 sq miles), Crete is sometimes called Megalónissos, or 'Great Island'. Visually it is stunning, with dramatic mountain ranges over 2,000m (6,500ft) high that seem to anchor the island in the sea. Water has cut vertiginous gorges through the mountains and gouged huge cave systems through their hearts. These caves were places of great religious significance to its ancient peo-

Crete is divided into four administrative provinces, named after their governing cities: Iráklio, the most populous, with the capital city; Haniá; Lasíthi; and Réthymno.

ples and thought to be the birthplaces of Greek gods. Over the centuries they provided protection for pirates, vagabonds and freedom fighters. Mountains were never conquered, even in the most recent fighting of the 20th century – their furthest valleys were too remote, their slopes too steep. Today, their peaks are the domain of numerous birds, including eagles and vultures.

Fertile plains and lowlands have been places to settle and farm since Neolithic times; abundant fresh spring water from the surrounding peaks helped ensure a rich harvest. Around the coastline – especially in the north – long sandy stretches brought tourists flocking from the advent of package tours, but variety exists here too, with several different coastal environments – rocky coves, tiny bays and marshy river tributaries.

The Fruitful Year

The seasons have true meaning on Crete. Springtime sees the hills awash with flowers and wheat crops ripening in the warming sun, kids are born and the goat flocks make the most of fresh pastures. As summer commences, the cereals are harvested and the land takes on an ochre hue. Birdsong gives way to the sound of cicada, and the smell of honeysuckle rises in the evening air. Midsummer sees Cretans seeking shade to escape the heat, while visitors head out in droves to top up their tans. The hollow clanging of goat bells can be heard across the

Crete exports fruits of all kinds, including oranges

countryside as flocks desperately search for sustenance in the parched hills.

Autumn brings a cooling of the temperature yet a warming of the landscape, as the colours mellow in the shallow arc of the late season sun. Stucco on buildings takes on a rosy hue, the grapes swell to tempting perfection, and gravity casts its wand over plump fruits. Soon, winter brings a blanket of snow to the mountains; wood smoke fills the air, and the old folks retreat to their warm hearths as crowds gather at the winter sports resorts. The olive harvest is the focal point of the year. This crop reigns

Goats are farmed in formidable numbers, for both milk and meat

supreme and millions of trees blanket hillside slopes and coastal plains, a symbol of man's reliance on the earth. It has sustained Cretans for too long to be treated with disdain.

The Cradle of Europe

The footsteps of history can be seen on every dusty path and urban street. Crete was the cradle of European civilisation, and the Minoans – a people believed to be mythological until evidence of their existence was confirmed in the early 20th century – travelled far and wide across the eastern Mediterranean for trade. A prodigious collection of artifacts now displayed in museums across the island shows them to be the first true European culture, whose lives were graced by art, sports and the pursuit of pleasure.

The Minoan civilisation suffered a sudden and terminal collapse in 1450 BC for reasons that have not been fully established. A devastating natural disaster was initially thought to be the cause, but archaeological theory now bends toward invasion by a warring people to be the most likely scenario. If this is the case, it heralded the start of thousands of years of invasion and subjection for the Cretans. Dorians, Athenians, Macedonians, Romans, Byzantines, Arabs, Venetians and Ottomans all came to take control. Evidence of their presence abounds in commanding fortresses, protective harbours, fine mansions, narrow winding alleys, elegant minarets and ornate fountains of the towns. In 1913 Crete finally achieved the long awaited *enosis* – union with its Orthodox homeland, Greece.

Freedom or Death

Cretans did not take kindly to their native land being usurped and, particularly in the years of Turkish occupation, they built a reputation as formidable and tenacious fighters, striking with speed and retreating to mountain strongholds to outwit their enemies. They took to the same lifestyle during World War II when Crete was invaded by German forces, fighting a successful guerrilla war and living up to the old rallying cry – 'freedom or death'.

The remains of Crete's first monastery, Katholikó

Invading forces could occupy the cities but they

could never manage to tame the people of the countryside. For centuries, unbowed Cretans lived simple lives in harmony with the land, tending their flocks, growing fruit and vegetables, and harvesting the sea. Clothes and carpets were made of wool, leather was used to make boots and saddles, wood was used for bowls and utensils, and grass and straw woven into basketwear. Seasonal gluts were preserved to provide sustenance for the long winters that often isolated mountain villages. The people put their trust in God, as the many Orthodox churches

El Greco was born in Fódele, Crete

across the island attest, praying for self-determination and for their sons and fathers hiding out in the hills.

Enduring Traditions

Although peace now reigns, a glance around communities in the Cretan heartland still suggests that little has changed. Whitewashed villages dot the landscape, each house with its own smallholding. The traditional diet – greens, olive oil, wild herbs, honey, yoghurt and a little lamb or goat meat – still sustains these rural people, and it has been scientifically proven to be one of the healthiest in the world. Men still stride out in the black breeches, leather boots and headscarves worn by previous generations; widows in black sit quietly crocheting in their doorways; and donkeys continue to perform duties in landscapes where modern vehicles are rendered useless.

If a Cretan's hatred of his enemy is legendary, it has always been surpassed by a generosity to his friends – and by extension to strangers (the Greek word for stranger and friend is the same). A door is always open to a passing traveller. Today, admiring an orchard of apples or a field of vines even in rudimentary Greek will result in an armful of fruit to take with you on your journey – just a small example of how tradition carries on through the generations. And how do today's Cretans find their pleasure? Poetry, literature, music and dance; traditional forms of all these arts are still alive and well here.

Yet despite all talk of tradition, Crete is also a very modern island, and Iráklio, the capital, a major Greek commercial town. You'll not escape the constant trill of mobile phones as people conduct business on the move or arrange

Conflict of Interests

Prosperity alters much that it touches. The difference in living standards, between those people directly benefiting from the tourist trade and those who are not involved, has in some cases led to social divisions. This happens today, not just around the coastal resorts, but inland, particularly as the newly enriched return to build opulent mansions in dilapidated ancestral villages.

But it would be a mistake to see only the negative side of tourism on Crete. There are no natural resources on the island and, apart from a few food and textile factories, no non-agricultural industry either. Jobs would be very scarce, if it were not for the tourist. One must hope that development is kept within reasonable limits, so that tourism will remain a blessing for visitors and islanders alike.

tonight's date. The contrast between the large coastal towns and the countryside is as great today as it has ever been. Young Cretans are just as interested in fashion and music as their continental cousins. They aim to find jobs with excitement, a secure future and ready cash to spend – something they feel a rural way of life cannot give them – and with a thriving commercial sector and vibrant intellectual scene, the capital exudes an urban confidence that surprises many visitors.

Of course the arrival of mass tourism has changed Crete, particularly along the northern coast where the

Mass tourism has changed the face of the north coast

majority of the development has taken place. The island is invaded by an annual army of tourists who flock here searching for sunshine, relaxation and fun; and Cretans seem happy to welcome everyone with precisely the kinds of activities that holidaymakers demand. However, there's just too much land and too much individuality here for Crete ever to become just another 'Euro-island'. Fears of a cultural meltdown, although perhaps understandable, are wide of the mark. Gritty and enduring as ever, Cretans will continue to do things their way. This cultural distinction, its fascinating history and the dramatic landscape will make Crete an enthralling holiday destination for generations to come.

A BRIEF HISTORY

Crete's long history is bound up with its strategic position at the crossroads between Western Europe, the Middle East and North Africa. In good times this brought trade, ideas and prosperity; in bad times, invasion, oppression and disease. Many fascinating legacies around the island attest to the complicated web that time has spun here, and each era has left its distinctive mark.

The earliest human remains found on Crete date back to the seventh millennium BC. The first inhabitants were Neolithic cave-dwellers who came from Asia Minor. These hunter-gatherers developed into farmers with settlements and pastureland on the fertile Messará Plain. It was an influx of new settlers with Bronze Age skills around 3000 BC that ushered in the Minoan era, the first major civilisation to arise on European soil.

The Minoans

A great ancient Cretan civilisation was for many years believed to be just the stuff of mythology. Yet with the discovery of marvellous artifacts and evidence of its cities, Sir Arthur Evans, its principal advocate, made reality out of folklore and myth *(see page 39)*. We now know many facts about Minoan Crete – including that, at the height of its influence, the population of the island probably numbered more than two million, approximately four times greater than today's figure, with 100,000 people living in the capital, Knossos.

> **Arthur Evans classified the three periods of Bronze-Age Crete as Early, Middle and Late Minoan. They are now known as the Pre-Palace, Old Palace and New Palace eras.**

A 3,500-year-old fresco of three Minoan women in Knossos

These early European settlements were built without fortifications and comprised vast numbers of dwellings. The cities developed ergonomically rather than to any grand design. The first palatial structures at Knossos, and other great cities such as Phaistos (modern Festós) and Malia, were erected around 2000 BC, but these were all destroyed by an earthquake 300 years later. The remains visible today are their replacements, even bigger and more splendid than the originals. The golden age for Minoan society – known as the New Palace era – lasted 300 years.

The Minoans were ruled by a priest-king who presided over both religious and economic affairs. It is unclear whether he reigned over the entire island, or if each palace settlement had its own regional king. His people worshipped the Mother Goddess, and divine power was symbolised by the bull, for whom they performed ornate and elaborate rituals. One sacred symbol, which is at odds with their peaceful

Exquisite gold jewellery from Malia, probably a burial offering

lifestyle, is the *labrys* (a double-headed sword). Its image has been found on various artifacts throughout the island.

The Minoans developed an alphabet and printing method, along with sophisticated plumbing and water-delivery systems. Women enjoyed high status, playing an active part in palace life, and the whole population enjoyed athletic contests, games and a whole range of recreational activities. Above all, they excelled in the visual arts.

Wherever there was a blank 'canvas' there was imagery: decorative entrances, walls, floors and pottery. Many breath-taking examples can be seen in the Archaeology Museum in Iráklio (*see page 34*). The smallest items, such as combs, were exquisitely worked. Gold and precious stones were fashioned into beautiful jewellery, all of which indicates a high quality of life for the people.

What fuelled this great empire was trade. Cretans exhibited their skills not only with local resources such as paint, clay, copper and bronze, but also with imported raw materials – lapis lazuli from Afghanistan, ivory from Syria, and gold, silver and black obsidian from Anatolia. Copper and bronze were worked and re-exported, along with high-quality foodstuffs such as olive oil, honey and wine.

The Minoans developed into one of the great naval powers of the Mediterranean, with the wood from the vast cypress forests providing material for boats. However, they concentrated their power more on commercial than military gain, showing a taste for the good life rather than a hunger for an empire.

This great civilisation came to a sudden, catastrophic end around 1450 BC. The exact cause remains unknown, but all the palaces were destroyed at the same time. The charred remains at Knossos and ash at Zákros suggest a great conflagration. A leading theory for many years was that natural disaster struck the island in the wake of the volcanic explosion on the island of Thíra (Santoríni), due north of Crete, bringing a maelstrom of tidal waves, earthquakes and fire storms. The most recent research has uncovered evidence supporting another hypothesis – that an attack by invaders or rebel forces may have brought about the end of this fine culture. Scholars will continue to debate the reason for many years to come.

Lató was the dominant city during the Dorian occupation

Dorians and Romans

After the disaster, Mycenaean Greeks from the Peloponnese moved in to control what remained of the Minoan settlements – they may even have precipitated the destruction. Around 1200 BC, Dorian invaders from the Balkans drove south through the Greek mainland, across the Aegean and into Crete.

Many coastal dwellers migrated to remote mountain villages in order to escape

The complex legal code of Gortys was carved in stone

their enemies. Others embarked on an overseas exodus that took them around the Mediterranean Sea. The island did not get directly involved in Greece's Persian and Peloponnesian Wars, although it became well known as a valuable source of brave and energetic mercenaries.

While mainland Greece was reaching its zenith during the Classical Age (480–338 BC), the island remained a backwater of warring city-states, of which Gortys (modern Górtyn) was the most powerful. Nevertheless, the enlightened Athenians acknowledged Crete as a source of much of their culture, and its caves and shrines were major centres of pilgrimage. The island's most important achievement – and only significant remnant – from this period is the law code of Gortys *(see page 44)*. It reveals a hierarchical society of free men, serfs and slaves ruled by an aristocratic class.

It took the Romans three years of brutal fighting to conquer Crete in 67 BC, and they did so only by playing the rival city-states against one another. Crete remained a province of the Roman Empire until AD 395, with Gortys as its capital. The Romans managed to bring a certain order to the island, putting an end to internal struggles, building new roads, ports and aqueducts, and introducing systems of domestic plumbing and central heating not much worse than those found today.

Early Christians

The apostle Paul arrived in AD 59 with his disciple Titus, whom he left behind to convert the islanders to Christianity. Titus had a hard time combating the Cretans' pagan beliefs, and was martyred for his overzealous efforts. But Christianity eventually triumphed to achieve the strong Orthodoxy of today, and Titus became Crete's patron saint.

When Roman power split in two, the eastern Byzantine Empire inherited the island (though its hold on islands in the south of its dominion were, in reality, nominal). Attacks by pirates and Islamic forces brought terror to the people, but Cretans remained loyal to the Orthodox Church throughout the Arab occupation of AD 824–961. The island was recaptured after a terrible siege of Iráklio by Byzantine commander Nikefóros Fokás. He catapulted the heads of dead Arabs into the city to dishearten those still defending the citadel.

> **The Greek Orthodox Church has always played a special role on Crete. Under foreign domination, the Church funded and organised schools where Greek history and traditions were taught and kept alive. Most significantly, it was the focus of unity and resistance to oppression, as indicated by the many attacks on Crete's 34 monasteries.**

Venetian Days

After Byzantium fell to the Crusaders, Crete was given to their leader, Boniface of Montferrat, who immediately

Icon painting in the Byzantine style flourished under the Venetians

sold it to Venice for 1,000 silver marks, ushering in a new era. Crete prospered greatly under the 465 years of Venetian occupation (1204–1669), although there were revolts by the native population, which were brutally put down. As a source of shipbuilding timber in a key location, the island was a kingpin in the far flung commercial empire, and became the Republic's first formally constituted overseas colony.

Proudly emblazoned with the Lion of St Mark, the ports and fortifications of Iráklio (called Candia under Venetian rule, as was the whole of Crete), Haniá and Réthymno bear witness to the Venetians' ambitious public building programme. Several handsome villas and loggias still attest to their gracious style of living.

Gradually Cretans settled down to intermarry with the occupiers and to participate in their style of government.

The arts flourished during the 16th and 17th centuries, a period known as the Cretan Renaissance. Numerous new monasteries and churches were built. Icon painting was at its height with an influx of artists from around Byzantium who founded important schools of art. The great literary figure of the time, Vitzéntzos Kornáros, wrote a romantic epic poem in the Cretan dialect, *Erotókritos*. Even if it has since lost its traditional hold in the mountain villages, it is still acclaimed among the literati of Crete.

The Battle for Crete

In the east, Christian forces were in retreat as a new Muslim power began to rise. The Ottoman Turks pushed Venetian and other forces from Asia Minor, through the islands of the Aegean, until they had left the Greek mainland. Eventually it would be Crete's turn. The Turks waged a titanic war to wrest the island from the Venetians. It began with raids on Haniá and Sitía in the 1530s by the notorious pirate Barbarossa Khair el-Din. Over the next century, the Venetians greatly strengthened the fortifications, but Haniá and Réthymno fell in 1645.

Two years later, the Turks laid siege to the capital, Candia. It was an epic struggle, which was to last 22 years. Initially

---

The Cretan Renaissance

After the fall of Constantinople in 1453, Crete became a haven for artists and theologians fleeing the Turks. A religious college for the study of painting, theology and the humanities was established at the Church of St Catherine in Iráklio *(see page 33)*, which became the centre of the Cretan Renaissance during the 16th and 17th centuries. El Greco is said to have studied here, along with his contemporary Mihaíl Damaskinós, and Vitzéntzos Kornáros, the author of the epic poem *Erotókritos*.

The Cretan artists excelled at icon painting, blending traditional Byzantine style with Venetian influences of Renaissance Italy. Their work was in demand throughout the Western world. Damaskinós, who worked in Venice from 1577 to 1582, was the master of this art. His use of colour and perspective brought a depth to the icon tradition that was widely imitated.

weakened by an outbreak of plague, the 12,000-strong population rallied to the cause. After 15 years, the Turkish commander, Hussein Pasha, was summoned back to Constantinople and publicly strangled for his failure to take the city. It is said that 30,000 defenders died, but there were 118,000 fatalities among the besiegers.

Although Western Europe's leaders watched with bated breath, they sent little support, and inexorably Venetian resistance was worn away. As the conquerors entered the city gates in 1699, the Venetians negotiated an orderly departure, taking with them, among other Christian artifacts, the cherished head of St Titus. This most symbolic of Crete's religious relics was not to return to the island until 1966.

Turkish Rule

Crete's years spent under the Turks (1669–1898) constituted a period of cultural and economic stagnation. Ottoman leaders had no interest in developing or investing in their dominions and, after the occasionally oppressive but often brilliant centuries of Venetian government, Crete slid back into the dark ages.

Apart from repairing the islands' fortifications, the Ottomans left few lasting remnants of their rule. They built very few mosques, preferring instead to convert existing churches, and left only a few houses. Most numerous of their legacies are the ornate street fountains found in the corners of market squares and outside chapels.

> **Crete celebrates its National Day on 8 November, the anniversary of the explosion in 1866 at Arkádi Monastery, where hundreds of Cretan rebels died rather than surrender to the Turks.**

There were sporadic attempts at revolt, which were often launched from remote mountain strongholds where

Monastery of martyrs: Arkádi is a shrine to Cretan resistance

rebels could survive in safety. The more vulnerable communities on the lower plains paid a high price for these revolts in the form of swift bloody reprisals. The first major rebellion occurred in 1770 when the Russians, hoping to distract the Turks while they waged their own attacks on the Ottoman Empire elsewhere, promised support to Daskalogiánnis, a wealthy shipowner. He raised a revolt in Sfakiá, but the support never arrived. The rebellion was crushed, Daskalogiánnis was flayed alive, and the event became the subject of a rousing epic poem.

There were notable uprisings in 1828 when the leaders were killed at Frangokástello, and in 1866 when hundreds of Cretans – and many Turks – died in a suicide explosion at Arkádi Monastery. It is not surprising that at this time many town-dwelling Cretans kept a low profile. They publicly converted to Islam to escape heavy taxes, continuing to practise their Orthodox faith in secret.

However, once Greece had achieved independence from the Ottoman Empire after the War of 1821, the atmosphere changed. Though Crete had to endure nearly a century more of subjection to Turkish domination, it stirred the blood of many native sons who vowed to rid the island of its oppressors. The ferocity of later Cretan resistance against the Turks had all the trademarks of their fiercely independent spirit. Violent insurrections provoked equally violent massacres in retaliation; and death came to form a monumental collective badge of honour.

The island's repeated suffering was duly celebrated in the popular, heroic *Songs of Digenis* (adapted from their medieval origins for the modern struggle), Pandelís Prevelákis' particularly grim novel *The Cretan*, and the lofty writings of Níkos Kazantzákis.

Union with Greece

Finally, in 1898, the European powers forced the Turks to grant Crete autonomy within the Ottoman Empire and accept Prince George, second son of the Greek king, as governor. This did not satisfy the

Elevthérios Venizélos, the Cretan who brought union with Greece

people and the prince resigned only a few years later under threat of revolt and the demand for union with Greece. It was only in 1913, under the leadership of the Cretan Elevthérios Venizélos, that the longed-for *énosis* (union) was achieved.

Despite being unscathed by World War I, Crete saw major changes in the mid-1920s. The Atatürk revolution, which announced a new Turkish Republic, brought massive upheaval through the area with a forced population exchange between Greece and Turkey beginning in 1923. Thousands of Turks were evacuated, and thousands of Greek refugees from Asia Minor arrived to take their place.

However, agricultural resources and output were improved and the new arrivals soon began to settle. The new science of archaeology was also developing, and excavations of Minoan palaces brought a new prosperity as the 20th-century phenomenon of tourism grew.

The dead of two world wars lie in Haniá's British War Cemetery

War and Peace

Yet Crete's pains were not yet over. During World War II, the rapid advance of the German forces through mainland Greece in 1941 forced the Allies to retreat to Crete. On 20 May, German troops invaded the island and secured the airfield at Máleme, situated to the west of Haniá. British, Australian and New Zealand soldiers joined Cretan militia during a valiant defence in the ten-day Battle of Crete, but were ultimately forced to retreat across the island. Many locals were evacuated to Egypt, though several thousand were left stranded and fled to the mountains. Casualties on both sides were terrible: Allied losses numbered 2,000 killed and 12,000 taken prisoner, while the German war cemetery contains almost 4,500 graves.

With their tradition of resistance to foreign invaders, Cretans kept up constant guerrilla warfare against the occupying Axis force. Efforts to shelter the Allies and smuggle them off the island in small groups from isolated south-coast beaches were remarkably successful. But the German army took brutal reprisals on the civilians. In 1944 the resistance pulled off an amazing coup by kidnapping the German commander, General Kreipe, and smuggling him off the island. German troops later marched through the Amári Valley, burning villages to the ground and killing any men they could find. The occupation of Crete did not end until May 1945.

Much of the island was left in ruins from heavy bombing, but Crete escaped the internal strife of the civil war that raged in mainland Greece (1947–9) and felt fewer effects of the oppressive 'rule of the colonels' (1967–74) than other Greek communities. Relative calm now reigns on the political front, and Greece's economic prospects have strengthened since it joined the European Community in 1981. In the same year, Andréas Papandréou, with strong support from Crete, led his PASOK party to victory and formed Greece's first socialist government.

Papandréou became prime minister with Cretan support

Crete, which till the 1950s was almost exclusively agricultural, has seen profound changes, and has been a beneficiary of Greece's huge increase in tourism. Today, it is one of the most prosperous regions of the country.

Historical Landmarks

6500–2600 BC Stone Age settlers arrive in Crete from Asia.

2600–2000 BC Pre-Palace era: more immigrants bring copper and pottery.

2000–1700 BC Old Palace period: discovery of bronze; language written down; first palaces built, then destroyed by an earthquake.

1700–1450 BC New Palace era: the golden age of Minoan civilisation.

c.1450 BC Minoan palaces destroyed; Mycenaeans arrive.

c.1200 BC Iron Age Dorians from northern Greece conquer most of Crete.

10th–1st centuries BC 'Dark Ages': Crete is ignored by Classical Greece.

67 BC–AD 337 Crete becomes a Roman province, with Gortys the capital; Titus brings Christianity.

337–826 Roman Empire splits, Crete falls to Byzantium (Constantinople).

824–961 Arabs conquer Crete, destroy Gortys, make their capital at fortress of Rabdh el-Khandak (Iráklio).

961 Nikefóras Fókas recaptures Crete for Byzantium.

1204 Venetians acquire Crete, rule for 465 years from Candia (Iráklio).

15th–16th centuries Crete the centre of Byzantine art and scholarship.

17th century Ottoman Turks gradually conquer Cretan cities.

1669 Turks capture Candia after 22-year seige and control all Crete.

1770 Daskalogiánnis leads unsuccessful revolt against Turks in Sfakiá.

1821–7 Greek War of Independence; Crete still under Turkish control.

1866 Revolt at Arkádi culminates in explosion killing hundreds.

1897–8 European Great Powers occupy Crete, which becomes an autonomous principality within the Ottoman Empire.

1912–13 Greeks take Crete from Turks, it becomes part of Greece.

1923 Last Turks finally leave Crete, Greeks return from Asia Minor.

1941–4 Germany occupies Crete: heavy losses, villages destroyed.

1960s Tourist boom begins.

1967–74 Greece ruled by right-wing junta of colonels.

1972 Iráklio replaces Haniá as capital of Crete.

1981 Greece joins the European Union. First socialist government.

2002 The euro becomes the principal unit of currency in Greece.

2004 Greece hosts the Olympics in Athens.

WHERE TO GO

GETTING AROUND

Crete is a large island, so if you want to see a lot of what it has to offer, choose your itinerary carefully. Staying at a central base allows for excursions to both the east and west, whereas a base in the far east or west limits your ability to see the opposite end of the island.

This guide divides Crete into four sections: first the capital, Iráklio, followed by the central section; then we move east, before finally exploring the western parts of the island. The major attractions are covered, so that you can plan your itinerary around them, but do remember that the countryside is filled with hidden treasures; traditional communities, frescoed churches and mountain paths. All of these are waiting to be discovered.

IRÁKLIO

Iráklio comes as a surprise to travellers used to Greek islands further north in the Aegean Sea. It is a true city bustling with activity. The commercial and administrative heart of Crete, its streets are filled with bankers and business people. There is a lively young scene based around the university, and a sophistication to match other major Greek cities such as Athens or Thessaloníki. However, this is not the only facet of the city. Around the harbour you'll still find a fishing industry based on small family-owned boats, and in the narrow backstreets small workshops that still manufacture by hand. Although there are many modern buildings, these sit shoulder-to-shoulder with fine old mansions and are evidence of an older Iráklio, which is fascinating to explore. Take time to see beyond the streets filled with traffic and you will be amply rewarded.

Iráklio was a thriving port in Minoan times and became known as Herakleium under Roman rule. The arrival of the Venetians changed the town's fortune. They chose it as their capital, giving the name Candia to both the city and the whole island. Candia blossomed with the riches of Venetian trade, and when Turkish forces stormed the island, the town held out for months before falling into Muslim hands. It became a relative backwater of the Ottoman Empire, only to rise to prominence again following union with Greece. It was declared capital again in 1971, taking the title from Haniá in the west.

The City Centre

The city centre lies within the walls of a vast fortress started by the Venetians and reinforced by the Turks. It is possible to walk along the walls to gain an impression of how large the citadel once was. The heart of the city is the tiny **Venizélos Square** (Platía Venizélou), with its fringe of cafés and restaurants. At its centre, the **Morosini Fountain** dates from Venetian times, though the sombre lion statues are 300 years older. From this square – known to tourists as Lion Square – most of Iráklio's attractions are only a few minutes' walk.

South, on 25 August Street (Odós 25 Avgoústou), you will see the impressive façade of the **Venetian Loggia**, originally dating from 1628 but reconstructed after a later earthquake. It now houses Iráklio's City Hall. Walk through the loggia to find the **Church of Ágios Títos**. Founded at the end of the first millennium, it is named in honour of St Titus, the island's patron saint who was charged by St Paul to convert the Cretans to Christianity. When the church was consecrated, Titus's body was laid to rest within the walls. The Venetians took his remains to Venice when they fled the island, and the church was rebuilt as a mosque after an earthquake in 1856, giving the incongruous but beautiful decoration on the outer walls. In 1966 the Venetian authorities returned the skull of St

The Koúles fortress stands guard over the Venetian harbour

Titus to the Cretan people in a gold reliquary, along with fine paintings depicting scenes of the saint's life. They are now on view inside. Head across 25 August Street to a small park – **El Greco** – named after the painter, a native of Crete, whose real name was Doménikos Theotokópoulos. Here you can sit under the shade of the trees away from the noise of the traffic.

The Harbour

Continuing along 25 August Street leads to the waterfront and the majestic sight of the **Venetian fortress** (Koúles; open Mon–Sat 8am–6pm, Sun 10am–3pm), built to protect the old harbour. You'll also see the vaulted remains of large arcaded *arsenáli* (ship repair yards) that serviced the Venetian fleet. The fortress sits out on the breakwater, and you will walk past the city's fishing fleet to reach it. Small colourful boats with piles of yellow nets are waiting to set sail for the next day's catch. The fortress was completed in 1540 to protect the town against the Ottoman threat. It proved a fine defence and explains how Candia held out for so long in the siege of the city throughout the 1660s. A tour of the interior reveals a strong and efficient design. There are wonderful panoramic views of the city and the surrounding countryside from its ramparts.

A short walk west along the waterfront brings you to the remains of the Dominican **Monastery of Ágios Pétros** (St Peter), which is currently in the process of renovation. Beyond this is the **Historical Museum of Crete** (open Mon–Fri 9am– 4.30pm, Sat 9am–2pm), housed in an impressive building that is part Venetian mansion, part modern glass edifice. The museum concentrates on Cretan history from the fall of the Roman Empire to the present. There are exquisite icons and other religious paintings rescued from churches across the island, stone carvings and examples of textiles and embroidery in a re-creation of a traditional Cretan home. Models and prints of Iráklio across the centuries show how the cityscape has developed. The struggle for Cretan independence is given a prominent position in the museum, as is the only painting by El Greco still on Crete.

Iráklio was first named Herakleium by the Romans, before the Arabs changed its name to Rabdh el-Khandak. Then the Venetians renamed it Candia. During the Turkish occupation, the Cretans called it Megalo Kastro ('big fortress'), until the official name Iráklio was adopted in 1922.

South of the City Centre

South of Venizélos Square is **1866 Street** (Odós 1866), also known as Market Street, which still has the atmosphere of an old Turkish bazaar. Here you can stroll past stalls selling fresh produce and souvenirs, or eat at the numerous ouzeries that serve the market workers. At the southern end of Market

Street is **Kornárou Square** (Platía Kornárou) where you will find the **Bembo Fountain** (Kríni Bembo) created in the 16th century using numerous pieces of architectural salvage, including the torso of a Greco-Roman statue.

A short walk from here to the left along the inner arterial road brings you to **St Catherine's Square** (Platía Agías Ekaterínis) where the 19th-century Cathedral of Ágios Minás dwarfs two older religious buildings. The small church immediately next to it is the **Church of Ágios Minás**, which has a splendid ornate iconostasis –

The market on 1866 Street

if the church is closed ask in the cathedral as the custodian here has the key. Behind these two churches is the 15th-century place of worship that gives the square its name: the **Church of St Catherine** (Agía Ekateríni). The church originally belonged to the religious community of St Catherine's monastery in the Sinai (now part of Egypt) and it acted as a centre of learning. Today it houses the **Museum of Icons and Sacred Objects** – a wealth of art from churches and monasteries across the island, including six large icons by the celebrated Cretan artist Mihaíl Damaskinós.

The Archaeological Museum

Walk east from Lion Square along the pedestrian street of Dedálou (Odós Dedálou) to reach the city's top attraction, the **Archaeological Museum of Iráklio** (open Tues–Sun 8am–7pm, Mon 12.30–7pm, Nov–Mar daily to 5pm). This is without a doubt one of the greatest archaeological collections in the world and it brings together finds from sites right across the island and from every era of Crete's ancient history, shedding light on the everyday activities of its people. Pride of place has to go to the Minoan artifacts. As the pre-eminent centre of this ancient people, Crete is the main source of information and excavated remains. The best finds from all Minoan sites are on display here.

> **In 1979 Prime Minister Karamalís wanted to loan part of the Minoan collection abroad. The people took to the streets armed, to protest against the removal of their historical art treasures from the Archaeological Museum of Iráklio.**

For the majority of other museums this would be treasure enough, yet in Iráklio there are also impressive Greek and Roman artifacts to enjoy. The museum is a must for those intending to visit the ancient sites, since the objects here add life to the now-empty cities and palaces.

To fully appreciate its glories will take at least a couple of hours – the exquisite detail in painting on pottery and frescoes, and the fine workmanship in jewellery and everyday tools is breathtaking. Try to visit early to avoid the large tour groups who arrive at midday. The 20 rooms are arranged in chronological order, grouping artifacts from each site. Below are some of the highlights you will discover on your tour.

Room 1 has the earliest finds, dating from 6000 BC (Neolithic and Pre-Palace periods). Many were found at Móchlos on the northeastern coast. Primitive pottery is on display here – including a rather naïve clay bull with an acrobat holding one horn – and finer work such as a stone *pyxis* (jewellery box) incised with geometric patterns and a reclining animal.

Room 2 is the first of two rooms displaying finds from the Old Palace period (2000–1700 BC), including the earliest examples of fine Kamáresware pottery, with its polychrome decoration, found in the ruins at Knossos. Fascinating miniature work is also in evidence, with a series of tiny faience plaques depicting the façades of Minoan houses.

Room 3 holds the Phaistos Disc, a clay disc 16cm (6¼in) in diameter, imprinted with hieroglyphic and geometric symbols that have yet to be deciphered. All the other finds here were also uncovered at the Phaistos Palace.

Room 4 has finds from the golden age of Minoan society – the New Palace period (1700–1450 BC). Artifacts originated in the palaces of Knossos, Mália and Phaistos and include the superb *rhyton* (libation vessel used in ritual

Double oil jars decorated in the floral style, from the New Palace period

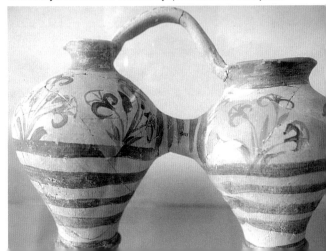

purification) carved from black steatite in the shape of a bull's head. The bull was one of the foremost religious symbols of the Minoans and this artifact was created by one of the pre-eminent artisans of the time.

Room 5 holds objects from the final phase of Minoan civilisation (1450–1400 BC). The pottery and stonework is worth studying, but the chief artifacts are the script fragments of Linear A type scribed on thin clay plates and not yet deciphered. Also exhibited are examples of Linear B type, which was deciphered in 1952 and is of Mycenaean origin – showing that by the time the tablet was written the Minoans had lost control of the major cities.

Room 6 concentrates on tomb finds that date from the New Palace and Post Palace periods. Items on display include beautiful pottery pieces, military artifacts such as helmets and sword handles, and splendid gold jewellery.

> **The highlight of Room 7 is case 101, which displays gold jewellery of exquisite detail, including the famous bee pendant found near Mália (see picture, page 16).**

Room 7 concentrates on domestic utensils and personal objects found in the palaces and around the *Megara* (royal chambers). These include stone vessels, pottery, hammers and a potter's wheel. There are several intricately carved steatite vessels, including the Harvesters Vase discovered at Agía Triáda and decorated with a low relief of men at work in the fields.

Room 8 is devoted to the palace of Zákros in the far east of Crete. The 'marine' amphora is decorated with octopuses and Argonauts. A delicate rock crystal *rhyton* on display here shows the sophistication of both workmanship and personal taste in the New Palace period.

Room 9 has finds from other sites in eastern Crete before room 10 moves on to the Post Palace period (1400–1100 BC), with pieces decorated in Mycenaean style. Rooms 11 and 12 concentrate on the period between 1100 BC and 650 BC, including a large collection of gold jewellery. Room 13 contains a number of painted Minoan sarcophagi, many decorated with the images of fish or birds.

Rooms 14 to 16 on the second floor display the finest remaining frescoes found throughout the Minoan kingdoms dating from 1600 to 1400. There are 21 in room 14, and nine in room 15, depicting the enigmatic Minoans at work and play, and their major influences – the bull, other animals and the marine environment. At the centre of gallery 14 is the only stone sarcophagus found on the island (at Agía Triáda). Spiral decoration frames scenes of libation and other religious activities. At the far end of the hall you can examine a miniature re-creation of the palace of Knossos, completed according to early hypotheses on its design.

The Agía Triáda sarcophagus shows tributes imported from Africa

Room 17 houses a once private collection – that of Irakliot doctor Stylianós Giamalákis – which came to the state in 1962. He obtained objects from every era of Crete's history, from Neolithic figurines to jewellery from the Venetian and Turkish eras. In addition there are objects of ancient Babylonian and Persian origin. Rooms 18 to 20 move on through the Archaic period to the Classical, Hellenistic and Roman eras, with colossal marble statuary gracing the gallery space.

However long you spend browsing this fantastic collection, you are sure to need some refreshment when you have finished. The museum has a café and there are several more just across the street from the entrance. Also here is the busy main tourist office.

CENTRAL CRETE

Central Crete is the market garden of the island, with fertile valleys sitting between rocky mountain ranges. Today it supplies much of the fresh produce for the population, including tons of grapes for the quaffable Cretan country wine. This is not a recent development: it was home to the Minoans, with their most famous palace only a few kilometres away from Iráklio. The Roman capital was also located in this region. Around these important archaeological sites are farming communities quite different in character from the city and the coastal resorts. Spend a little time exploring these villages for a glimpse of a lifestyle that will soon disappear as the younger generation turns its back on a rural way of life.

Vines in abundance near Iráklio

Knossos

Just five kilometres (3 miles) south of Iráklio is **Knossos** (open daily 8am– 7pm, winter to 5pm), now famed worldwide as the village where Sir Arthur Evans (at that time Director of the Ashmolean Museum in Oxford) found proof that the Cretan civilisation of myth had been based on reality. Evans named them the Minoans after their most famous king – Minos. He began digging in 1900 after buying the site and financing the excavation programme with his own money, and almost immediately struck the first building blocks of a huge Bronze Age palace

The Minoan palace at Knossos is Crete's foremost tourist attraction

replete with magnificent pottery and other artifacts.

Evans' subsequent attempts to re-create areas of the palace have met with intense criticism from other scholars but Knossos is now Crete's premier attraction, and rightly so. Although there is no documented proof, the majority of Cretans believe that Knossos was the site of the famed battle between Theseus and the Minotaur in the Labyrinth below King Minos's palace. You may wish you had a ball of golden thread as you explore the maze of small rooms here, as it is very difficult to follow the map provided. It also becomes extremely busy in the middle of the day, so arrive early if you want to view the site before it gets too hot and crowded.

The first palace at Knossos was built c.2000 BC in the Old Palace era, but this was destroyed by a massive earthquake only 300 years later. Most of what you see at the site today are the remains of the second palace, built following the disaster. This coincided with a golden age of Minoan society (the New Palace era, from 1700 BC), when the people grew rich through trade, and artistic endeavour was at its peak. The palace expanded continuously through the following years resulting in a complex of around 1200 small rooms several stories high covering over 20,000 sq m (215,280 sq ft). The construction was immensely complicated with light wells illuminating lower chambers and *polythyra*, masonry supports to create structural integrity, between which were large wooden doors serving as partitions.

The golden era came to an end in 1450 BC, and major fire caused catastrophic damage around 1350 BC, but though the palace was completely destroyed, the site continued to be occupied until the 5th century AD.

The palace was erected around a large **Central Court**, used for public meetings, which now forms the heart of the site. Imagine Minoans at play here as depicted on the pottery and frescoes in the Archaeological Museum in Iráklio – acrobats and dancers as well as the famed bull leapers. Visitors enter past what remains of the **West Court**, used as an entryway to a **West Wing,** where the administrative and religious activities took place. Minoans would walk down the corridor of processions past frescoed walls to reach the *propylaia* (sacred entranceway). A **Grand Staircase** then led north to the most important official chambers within this wing, its sturdy painted colonnades typical of those found throughout the palace.

The lower floor here houses the **throne room**, with ornate griffin frescoes and a lustral basin for ritual purification. The gypsum throne is the oldest in Europe, and

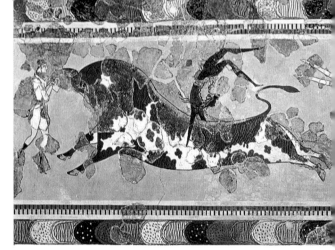
The famous 'bull-leaping' fresco shows a daring acrobatic game

traces of paint show that it would have been brightly coloured when in use. The walls – lined with stone seats thought to have been used by advisers or councillors – would have been decorated with red plaster and an ornamental dado. In the northeastern corner was a crypt where a cache of treasures was unearthed during the excavations.

A staircase by the throne room leads to what Evans christened the *piano nobile* – an upper floor of the west wing. Next to the staircase is the **Tripartite Shrine** where the Linear B alphabetical tablets were discovered.

On the east side of the court, a grand staircase leads to the royal chambers or *Megara*, where some of the best preserved rooms can be found. Notice the clever use of lighting wells to illuminate the lowest stories (there were four in total). The **King's Megaron** is decorated with a simple wooden throne, although the antechamber walls are incised with images of the double axe or *labrys*, so important to the mythology surrounding Knossos. The room is also known as the **Hall of the Double Axes**. The architecture of this room is typically New Palace style with large *polythyra* supporting the roof. It is thought that large wooden doors were fitted between the pillars and that these could be removed to create a *stoa* (open-fronted arcade), if the king wished it. The **Queen's Megaron** has a splendid dolphin fresco lining one wall.

Evans made numerous remarkable finds at the site, since it had been covered and left undisturbed following the 1350 BC disaster. Pottery intricately painted with marine life, bronze figurines and exquisite jewels – many of these were discovered in the rock cut tombs of Palace period. Yet it is the mundane and simple things that make Knossos so fascinating. Evidence of early water piping, central heating and sanitation shows a remarkable sophistication – look for the toilet room next to the Queens chamber for evidence of a flushing system. Continue past the remains of a hypostyle hall, which was the Customs House, to the start of the Royal Road lead-

---

Rites and Sacrifices

In the Minoan civilisation, the bull symbolised virility and all natural forces. The walls of the palace of Knossos are covered in paintings and sculptures of huge sacred horns. In the courtyard, young people used to perform an acrobatic game where they had to grab the bull's horns and leap above the animal. Every year, a bull was caught, its throat slit and its blood collected. This sacrifice bound the Minoan society and the animal's divine powers in the great cycles of nature. The Mother Goddess was represented by the Snake Goddess's bare breasts, a symbol of fertility. The snake itself was a symbol of reincarnation and healing. The sacred pillar embodied the goddess, while the double-headed axe represented the moon and the double power – religious and political – of the priest-king.

ing north to the coast, still in exceptional condition and far better than the majority of thoroughfares on Crete until only a few years ago.

On the road to Knossos, look for the **Natural History Museum of Crete** (open daily 9am–8pm) – an often-overlooked attraction but worth a visit for those interested in geology, flora and fauna. Exhibits concentrate on endemic species and the

Huge jars called *píthi* were used to store grain, oil, wine or water

diverse environments in Crete. It also examines man's effect on the island from his earliest arrival to the present day.

Towards Gortys

Other Classical sites lay below Iráklio near the south coast. Take the road to **Agía Varvára**, in a vine-filled valley skirting the looming mountains of the Ida range to the west. Here you'll find the **Mesará Plain**, a wide fertile valley surrounded by hills and a centre for farming since ancient times. For a pretty drive along the upper reaches of the valley, take the road to **Zarós** from Agía Varvára. The scenery is magnificent and you can visit **Moní Vrondisíou**, a small monastery in the hills above the town; this was the original home of the Damaskinós icons, which are now in Agía Ekaterínis in Iráklio. This road leads through the villages of **Kamáres** where there is a large cave, and links up with the Amári Valley to the west (see page 73).

To reach the ancient sites drop down from Agía Varvára on to the plain. Near the village of **Ágii Déka** – named after ten saints who were martyred here – and widely scattered in

farmland, are the remains of **Gortys** (Górtyn), capital of the
island during the Roman era (from 65 BC) and also an important
city in Minoan times.

Gortys is such a huge site – at its height it had a population
of 300,000 – that you will see signposts to remains lying in
the midst of crops south of the modern road. By all means,
stop to enjoy them, or leave the car in the village and walk
around. You'll be well rewarded, with ancient columns resting
against olive trees, shards of pottery among the grass
blades, and a governor's palace and amphitheatre to explore.
Stop at the Byzantine church in the village – you'll find
stone from the ancient site used here too – and see the stone
execution block of the martyrs. Their tomb can be viewed
through the gate of a nearby crypt.

The main site (the one with the admission fee, open daily
8am–7pm) covers only a tiny part of the whole, but it protects
one of the most important archaeological finds on the island –
the **Code of Laws** dating from the Dorian period, around 500
BC. The huge stone tablet was incised with script dictating
codes governing daily life including rules on marriage, prop-

---

Kamáres Pottery

Kamáres vases date from the Early Palatial Period, deriving their
name from where they were found, the Kamáres caves on the southern
side of the Ida Mountains. The characteristic features are polychrome
paintings on a dark background. Motifs from nature such as
spirals and rosettes combine to create a harmonious unity.

Late Palatial Period vases of the so-called floral style display
leaves or other plant motifs, while marine-style vessels are covered
with octopuses, paper nautilus or even coral designs. These vessels
were either buried with the dead, given as votive offerings or else
used as crockery in the palaces where they were found.

erty and inheritance rights. The remains of a small theatre lie just in front of the code area, and the site entrance is dominated by the apse of the 6th- century **Basilica of Ágios Títos** (St Titus). The remains of the saint were originally interred here but were moved to Iráklio following Arab raids which destroyed the remainder of the building in 825.

The remains of the 6th-century Basilica of Ágios Títos at Górtyn

Phaistos

Travel on through the village of Mires to reach **Phaistos** (Festós), the site of an impressive Minoan palace (open daily 8am–7pm summer, 8am–5pm winter). As Gortys rose in prominence towards the end of the first millennium BC, the fortunes of Phaistos declined, though it had been the seat of power for most of southern Crete in Minoan times.

Phaistos is probably the most dramatic Minoan site on the entire island. Its palace is set on top of a rocky knoll with rooms cascading down the hillside. There are dramatic views out across the plains to the Ída Mountains in the north and the Asteroúsia range in the east. It is said that King Minos installed his brother Rhadamanthys as ruler here. He was known as a wise and honest man consulted by many as an arbitrator.

The layout of the palace is similar to that of Knossos, though the remains are more confusing, with three successive palaces – two from the Old Palace era and one from the New Palace era – on show here. You enter the site down a flight of steps and find yourself in the **west court**. The remains in the

An ancient olive tree

foreground are those of the Old Palace, and stand proudly in front of the walls of the New Palace behind. You'll see scant remains of a shrine and early *propylon*. Above the shrine is a **grand stairway** leading to the *propylaeum*, the grand entryway into the New Palace. The **west wing** – as at Knossos – was chiefly made up of shrines and storerooms, and many objects of ritual were found during excavations here. You'll find that some rooms still house their lustral bowls for ritual purification. A path to your right leads down some steps and through a room to the central courtyard; from here you can get your bearings.

Walk to the **north court** where you enter the royal chambers – two giant *píthi* (large earthenware pots) guard the entryway from the central court. You'll find a peristyle hall here and steps leading down to the **King's and Queen's chambers** – both built to make the most of the cooling updrafts of the hillside. The east court was mainly used for practical activities, as there are remnants of a furnace and workshops here – perhaps for copper smelting. They would have supplied the palace with its need for ceremonial or funerary articles.

The **Phaistos disc** was discovered here in 1903 but not in any of the important Palatial-era rooms. It was found by workmen on the northern edge of the site in a tiny clay walled chamber. The disc, which is said to date from around 1700 BC, is covered with a spiral pattern of symbols and geometric forms that have yet to be deciphered. You can see the original in the Archaeological Museum in Iráklio; or buy a copy at any souvenir store.

Agía Triáda

Just 3km (2 miles) from Festós is **Agía Triáda**, built, archaeologists believe, as a summer palace for the royal court and linked to the city by Minoan road. Set on a hillside overlooking the Gulf of Mesará it offered excellent views and cooling sea breezes, as the sea came much closer in those days. The remains indicate a series of blocks of rooms that could work either as a whole or individually – perhaps to accommodate varying sizes of entourage at different times. The west wing housed the royal quarters.

Agía Triáda was built late in the Minoan era, c.1700 BC and although it suffered great damage in the cataclysm of 1450 BC, it was reoccupied, and a Dorian town was built nearby. Since this was famed in its time for several shrines, scholars have debated that the original palace may have had some religious purpose. Numerous tombs have been excavated on the hillside, and the sarcophagi in the Iráklio museum, finely decorated with cult scenes, was found here. Atop the whole site is the incongruous **Ágios Geórgios**, a pretty whitewashed 14th-century church.

Agía Triáda and its mountains

Mátala beach viewed from one of the famous caves

Mátala to Agía Galíni

If by now you are in need of some rest and refreshment make your way to the coastal resort of **Mátala** just a little way southwest of Festós. Here you'll find a good sandy bay lined with tavernas, and you can enjoy a re-energising lunch or cool dip. The waters are well-regarded by snorkellers and there are fascinating remains of a Roman port under only a few feet of water. On the northern side are high sandstone cliffs where you will find many large **Roman tombs** cut into the rock. Until recently they were unprotected and used as free camping spots by travellers. Today these man-made caves are fenced and guarded, though you can still explore them for a small fee.

Another good spot for lunch is **Vóri**, north of Festós. This traditional village has a shaded central square with a couple of tavernas. There's a Folklore Museum near the village hall.

Travelling west from the archaeological sites you'll reach the coastal resort of **Agía Galíni**, its buildings tumbling down a hill to a tiny port from which you can take trips along the coast. North from Agía Galíni the main road leads to Réthymno *(see page 67)*.

The Central Mountains

Heading west out of Iráklio you can take the fast road (New National Road) along the coast, with easy links to the resorts of **Agía Pelagía** (with organised watersports), **Balí** and **Pánormos**, or take the slower Old National Road, which winds its way inland. Taking this road allows you to explore some of the most rugged and interesting landscapes in Crete, and leads you back to the time of Greek mythology, when the gods ruled the earth. The **Ida Mountains** (Óros Ídi, also known as the Psilorítis range) dominate central Crete, rising steeply from the coastal plain and crowned by **Mt Ida** (Ídi) itself, measuring a distinguished 2,456m (8,058ft). In summer they seem almost to touch the clear azure sky; in winter they attract a mantle of snow and swathes of thick menacing clouds, and the villages of their lower slopes seem to hang suspended on this grey swirling blanket.

The men and women of this region have been some of the most stalwart against Crete's enemies, and subject to some of their worst reprisals. One such village is **Anógia**. The population suffered two bloody beatings under the Turks when the village was razed to the ground, and again in World War II. When Cretan partisans kidnapped General Kreipe, head of the occupying forces on the island, the Germans unleashed a terrible reprisal here. Soldiers marched into the village killing all the men and razing houses to the ground. Several monuments in the village commemorate

There are more than 3,000 caves in Crete – approximately half of all the caves in Greece. This is due to the crystalline nature of the island's limestone crust.

the sad events. Through happier times the village has built a reputation for weaving and embroidery – still sold in the lower town – as well as for its *lyre* players, and this is one place where you are sure to see men in their traditional costume of high leather boots, breeches and headdress.

Anógia is the main point of entry to the higher mountains. Follow the road out of the top of the village and upward to the Nída Plateau, a land once visited only by shepherds tending their flocks. Continue through the barren wastes until you reach the tourist pavilion, where you can stock up on necessities such as water and snacks. There is a hotel here and a ski centre nearby, showing just how much times have changed. Beyond the hotel the road leads on to the Idaean Cave (Idéon Ándron) where it is said that Zeus – the god of all Greek gods – spent his childhood, protected from his father Kronos by fierce warriors, the *kouretes*. Though the cave itself is not impressive by Cretan standards, it held a powerful sway over its ancient people. It is even said that King Minos himself would travel here every nine years to receive new laws from above. Archaeologists have found votive offerings dating back over 3,000 years, attesting to the ancient power of the site.

Climbing Mount Ida takes around nine hours (round trip) from the Idaean Cave. It is advisable to take a guide; inquiring in Anógia should help you find one.

EASTERN CRETE

This part of Crete is a fascinating amalgam of landscapes. Some of the longest-established resorts expand along the northern coast, while the interior has verdant valleys dividing mountain ranges that were remote until very recently. Here, it is still possible to explore the traditional rural lifestyle once omnipresent in the interior of the island. Cave systems and ancient sites add to the attractions, and make the east a good location for a combination beach/excursion holiday.

Rowdy Resorts

Heading out from Iráklio you'll pass the airport some 5km (3 miles) away before reaching the beginning of the coastal strip. The New National road takes you swiftly along, so if you want to explore take the Old National road. Your pace will be slower but you'll see more. This part of the northern coast was the main area of development during the 1970s and '80s, and it is not to everyone's taste. Large concrete hotels and apartment buildings line the strip, and it's a home from home for many European nationals, with English, German and Dutch menus, satellite football and all the favourite northern European TV programmes. It's almost impossible to believe that you are on a Greek island. However, if you want almost nonstop fun, then this is the place for you. Water-parks, bungy-jumping, go-carting, bars and nightclubs – it's all here.

The bare mountains and verdant valleys of eastern Crete

A poolside bar in Mália

Mália

The development reaches a peak at **Liménas Hersonísou**, although the inland village of **Áno Hersónisou** still has vestiges of its old atmosphere – and some nice tavernas. Once past the good beaches of **Mália** it peters out, and has completely given way to farmland when, around 2km (1 mile) to the east, you reach the site of the **Minoan Palace of Mália** (open daily 8.30am–3pm).

Remains under and around the palace show Neolithic settlements, although the first palace was built after 2000 BC (later than Knossos and Phaistos) and it revealed no Kamáresware pottery from the Pre-Palace period like that found at the other palaces. Its design is also simpler, with no large halls or fine wall decorations. This first palace was destroyed by an earthquake c.1700 BC and there are scant remains of it left in the northwest of the site.

The new palace centred on an open courtyard with a **west wing** mainly consisting of magazines (storerooms) and cult rooms. A loggia fronted the square on this wing. In one room a *píthos* was found with a ceremonial dagger inside, and alongside this lay a sword decorated with gold and crystal, leading scholars to conclude that this was a preparation or contemplation room for the king. Up a nearby flight of stairs is an **altar room** with the base of its altar table still in situ.

Further west a *polythron* area with a paved floor is thought to have been the **royal apartments**. Hieroglyphic clay tablets and official seals were found here. Just a little way north of the palace site is the **chrysólakkas** or 'pit of gold', where the much-prized **'golden bee' pendant** was discovered among a greater cache of jewels.

Soon after Mália Palace the road turns inland past the town of **Neápoli**, birthplace of Pétros Phílargos who became Pope Alexander V in 1409. This is the only place on the island were you can try *soumáda*, a sweet drink made from almonds. Look for the **Chapel of Ágios Geórgios Selináris** on your right as you go up through the mountain pass. This shrine to safe passage along the road was once set high above the old road and was only accessible up a narrow rocky path. Today, it stands beside the new fast road and its prayers are perhaps most needed by those trying to cross from the opposite side to visit it.

The ruins of Mália's second Minoan palace

Ágios Nikólaos

Eventually the road meets the coast at **Ágios Nikólaos**, probably the prettiest town in eastern Crete. Though Ágios Nikólaos – known to everyone as 'Ag Nik' – suffered from a sudden rush of ugly buildings going up in the 1970s, and has a young and noisy crowd, it has made an effort to keep its character, and offers a more Greek atmosphere than the Mália/Hersónisou strip.

The town sits on the **Gulf of Mirabélou**, blanketing low hills which rise up from the shoreline. At the centre of town is **Lake Voulisméni**, a deep freshwater spring-fed lake where a plethora of pretty fishing boats are tied. Numerous cafés and tavernas line the north and eastern edges of the lake, and you can sit and watch the kingfishers swoop for minnows or divers descend to the blue/green depths. The south and west sides of the lake are flanked by sheer rock faces and you can climb the steps to the top for superb views over the town – perfect at sunset.

Lake Voulisméni is connected to the sea by an artificial channel. Across the road bridge at its mouth is the main tourist office, and beyond are the harbour and port. Sea breezes here often make this stroll cooler than around the lake. From the port you can take caïque (small colourful wooden boats) trips to nearby attractions, most notably Spinalónga Island.

Eastern Crete's prettiest town: Ágios Nikólaos

You won't be able to explore Ágios Nikólaos without walking up a few hills. There are shops selling up-market clothing around the harbourside and along Odós Skafianáki, to the west. Or take Odós Koundoúrou to Platía Venizélou for more typical Cretan souvenirs such as honey and ceramics.

The local **Archaeological Museum** (open Tues–Sun 8.30am–3pm, Aug–Sept to 5pm) found at the top of Odós K. Paleológou is worth a visit. It has a good collection of Minoan artifacts, presented in chronological order. You will be able to view a sarcophagus with skeleton still in place, and the Goddess of Mýrtos, a libation vessel dating from the 2nd millennium BC in the shape of a woman with a long neck and squat body. A later Roman find is the skull of Potamos, decorated with a crown of gold olive leaves. The coin nearby was found between the skull's teeth

Life is leisurely in Ag Nik

and is thought to be the dead man's fare for the ferry across the River Styx to the underworld.

Ag Nik does not have great beaches; as a consequence much of its up-market accommodation is outside the town. Head north and you'll find some of the best accommodation in Europe, with a cluster of luxury hotels at **Eloúnda**. The village itself is understated, with a pretty church on the waterfront. You can also head to Spinalónga from here – a much shorter trip than from Ágios Nikólaos because the island lies just offshore. Its lower section is linked to the mainland by a narrow bridge. Or you can head further north on the main island to the tiny coastal resort of **Pláka** and take a rowing-boat ferry to Spinalónga. You'll find a number of excellent seafood tavernas here for an alfresco lunch after your visit.

Spinalónga Island

Spinalónga Island has been settled since ancient times. In the shallows off its southern tip are the remains of the Greco-

Roman city of **Oloús,** and just beyond the bridge a 4th-century AD mosaic within the foundations of an early Christian basilica. But it is the north of the island that attracts most visitors. Here, on a small rocky sub-islet are the remains of the Venetian stronghold of Spinalónga, built in 1579 to protect the entrance to this sheltered bay. Its strong bastions and high 'curtains' were never taken by an enemy. The Venetian garrison remained here until 1715, over 60 years after the fall of Iráklio, and left only after a treaty gave them safe passage. The Turks in turn retreated to the island when they came under threat from Cretan rebels at the end of the 19th century.

> **Oloús was still a flourishing city in the 2nd century AD, according to Greek geographer Pausanias. It probably sank beneath the waves during tectonic upheavals in the 4th century.**

At the beginning of the 20th century, the Cretan council decided to open a leper colony on the island; whether this was an attempt to force the Turks to leave is open to debate, but the disease was rampant on the main island and Spinalónga's position – offshore yet not too remote – was considered ideal for study of the disease and a quarantine for its sufferers. Initially, the regime was harsh, with fear and ignorance causing victims to be treated more like criminals than patients; however, conditions improved over the years until the colony was disbanded in 1957. Wandering among the remains lends poignancy to your exploration. This history was made within the lifetime of many visitors.

Inland to Kritsá

Inland from Ágios Nikólaos are three attractions that make an enjoyable morning or afternoon sightseeing. Head out towards the village of Kritsá 12km (7 miles) from town. Before you reach the village itself you'll find a beautiful

Byzantine chapel on your right. **Panagía Kerá** was built in the 13th century and decorated with superb frescoes of the 14th and 15th centuries. You'll need time to take in every detail of the interior and the simple lines of the exterior.

Resume your journey toward Kritsá, but don't visit the village just yet. Instead, follow signs to **Lató**, the remains of a Dorian city (7th–3rd centuries BC) scattered around two scrub-covered hilltops to the north (open Tues–Sun 8.30am– 3pm). The blocks of strong stone do not rival the beautiful fresco-covered walls of Minoan settlements, but there is a satisfaction in both location and form when you climb among the remains of Lató. There are also spectacular views from here down to the coast.

Spinalónga's former leper colony

Finally, you can allow yourself to head into **Kritsá**, perhaps to take some well-earned refreshment. This 'traditional' village is perhaps overly touristy for some but it is still very much lived-in and extremely well kept, with brilliant whitewashed walls accented by brightly painted window frames and pretty potted plants. You'll find good tavernas around the old village square – distinguished by its huge plane tree. Always famed for its carpet weaving and textiles, you'll see examples hanging from walls and shop doorways in the narrow streets. There is an extensive range

The village of Kritsá is famed for its weaving

of Cretan handicrafts and traditional foodstuffs from which to choose, making Kritsá a good place to do your souvenir shopping.

The Lasíthi Plain

While Kritsá is a good example of the modern development of traditional Cretan lifestyle, you won't need to travel far from the coastal resorts to find a lifestyle hardly touched by the 21st century. Travelling inland toward the towering peaks of the **Díkti Mountains** brings you to a plateau that was cut off from the rest of Crete by all but donkey traffic until well after World War II. Improved access to the **Lasíthi Plain** now allows visitors to view one of the few remaining old agricultural lifestyles in Europe.

Two roads climb up to the 850m (2,800ft) plain. From Mália you can pass through the tiny settlement of **Krási** with a 2,000-year-old plane tree gracing the main square, and **Kerá**, where you can visit 14th-century **Panagía Kardiótissa** (Our Lady of the Heart) before proceeding through the dramatic **Séli Ambélou Pass**. Or you can rise from Neápoli through several small communities for a panoramic initial view of the plain and the impressive **Psarí Madára** peak (2148m/7047ft) beyond. One road links the small communities so you are sure not to miss any detail. Try to visit before noon or after 4pm, especially in summer, as most farming activity stops in the heat of the afternoon.

Shepherds watch their somnolent flocks; farmers hand weed their vegetable patches; laden donkeys make their way relentlessly towards home; at harvest time the smell of ripe grapes and apples fills the air – this is Lasíthi. The small settlements are almost ghostly silent save for the crochet needles of the old ladies or the clicking of old men's worry beads at the *kafeníon*. Stop in **Ágios Geórgios** to visit the **Folklore Museum** (open summer only, 10am–4pm) and look for the remnants of hundreds of small windmills that once powered water pumps. Now only a few still turn in the breeze, and irrigation is more high-tech.

On the southern edge of the plain is a large cave said to be the birthplace of Zeus – the **Dictean Cave** (Diktéon Ándron). Though no proof can be put forward to support this claim, judging from the ancient votives left in the cave it was certainly very important during Minoan times. It is a 15-minute walk from the parking lot, or you can take a mule ride up the narrow path. Be aware that the surface underfoot is very slippery, and take a flashlight for better visibility inside the cave. The cave drops precipitously 65m (215ft) into a dark cavern where the imagination begins to work overtime – what demons could lurk here? A guide will help to point out details that your untrained eye might miss – such as the monstrous face of Kronos here to eat his

Only a few of Lasíthi's many windmills still function

new offspring Zeus, and the small nipple-shaped stalagmites on which the infant god is said to have suckled.

The Dictean Cave is one of Crete's most popular excursions and is very busy in the peak of the day. The surrounding area is also replete with souvenir stalls and ceramics workshops that either spoil the view or delight the shopper, depending on your point of view.

East from Ágios Nikólaos

Heading east from Ágios Nikólaos, the road along the northern coast is in the long process of being updated. Follow the gulf south to **Ístro** where there is a cluster of hotels, and then on along the coastal plain to one of the major ancient sites in the east – **Gourniá**, 18km (11 miles) south of Ágios Nikólaos. Myriad stone walls – foundations for multi-storeyed homes – linked by cobbled streets blanket the hillside site of Gourniá. Here more than at any other site it is possible to envision ordinary Minoans going about their daily business. You'll be able to explore the marketplace and workshops of the artisans (open Tues–Sun 8am–7pm, Mon noon–7pm).

The palace sat at the top of the hill, its west court housing a sacrificial slab and magazines for the storage of ritual liquids and libations as seen in other Minoan palaces. Gourniá was a large city, stretching down to the coast where it had an important port. Much remains to be discovered under the low scrub and rocks, though there seems little intent to do so. The best overview of Gourniá – excavated by American Harriet Boyd Hawkes in the early 1900s – is from the main road as it rises beyond the archaeological site.

From Gourniá the road along the northern coast takes a series of switchbacks through the foothills of the Ornó Mountains. There are tantalising views of several mountain villages and it is well worth leaving the car to explore their upper reaches. Take a left turn down to the coast at **Móhlos**, now an easy-going village but during Minoan times an important site. The Minoan settlement sits on a small island just 150m (480ft) offshore – you can take a boat or swim across to reach it – although it was connected to the mainland 3,000 years ago. A little way offshore to the west is **Psíra,** for which you definitely will need boat transportation.

Eventually the northern road drops into **Sitía,** a bustling town of over 8,000 people, which benefits from its relative isolation from the main tourist resorts. Tavernas and waterfront cafés

Gourniá is the most completely preserved of all Minoan towns

cater much more to local clientele and the town makes a living from its busy port. The Minoan settlement of **Petrás** lies 1km (½ mile) to the east and it was the Venetians who made their town on this hillside location, building a fortress – the **Kazárma** – on its highest point. Unfortunately the Turks destroyed the old Venetian buildings when they took the town but a network of narrow lanes and stone steps spill down to a waterfront promenade, and these have delightful architectural and lifestyle details to discover. Sitía also has a pleasing **Archaeological Museum** (open Tues–Sun 8.30am–2.30pm) displaying finds from Petrás and Gourniá. You'll find it just south of the town centre.

Sitía is the gateway to the far east of Crete. Now sparsely populated, it is the site of several important Minoan sites suggesting that many people lived here 3,000 years ago. Today's settlements are small dusty villages only recently benefiting from electricity. Many farming families still endure a hard life on these low brush hills. For those who want to explore the area, accommodation can be rented in private rooms in the larger villages. Surprisingly, even in this remote part of the island a procession of tour buses arrives every day from Ágios Nikólaos and beyond.

One of Crete's most influential religious institutions, **Toploú Monastery** (Moní Toploú; open daily 9am–1pm,

2pm–6pm), is found here on a windswept hilltop, surrounded by large swathes of fertile land bequeathed to it by grateful believers. Founded in the 14th century, the monastery was built for contemplation, but also for protection against the very real threat of the Turks.

Toploú is a Turkish word meaning cannonball – the more correct title for the monastery is Moní Akrotirianí – and it gives an indication that the leaders were no timorous recluses. Its walls put one in mind of a fortress rather than a religious refuge – though even these were not enough to protect it against its enemies and it was sacked several times in its early history. The order played a great part in Cretan uprisings against the Turks – monks were hanged in 1821 – and more recently against the Germans in World War II when it was a rallying point for British soldiers and native partisans. The abbot and several monks were shot in reprisal before the war's end.

The monastery has many treasures within its church – Panagía Akrotirianí – and museum. Some 61 late-18th-century scenes based on the Greek prayer *Lord, Thou Art Great* by renowned icon painter Ioánnis Kornáros are among the highlights, along with jewel-encrusted vestments and reliquaries of precious metals. You can visit the simple monks' cells

Tiers of colour-washed houses rise from Sitía's tree-lined waterfront

Toploú: a peaceful monastery with a bloody history

on the first floor and explore the old flour mill, which once brought income to the order. Today, the farmland owned by the monastery produces organic olive oil considered some of the best on Crete. You can buy it at the small gift shop along with icons and religious books.

Northeast of Toploú is one of Crete's natural wonders. Amid this arid landscape an oasis of verdant palms come into view and beyond a swathe of white sand ringing azure waters. This is **Vái**, which is extremely beautiful and very popular at the height of the season. The palms are said to have grown from stone spat out by Arab pirates during the first millennium, but today's crops are not edible.

South of Toploú the road sweeps on to the modern village of **Palékastro** and its nearby ancient site of the same name, then doglegs south to **Zákros** where you can leave the car and hike to the coast down one of the most dramatic gorges in the east, the **Valley of the Dead**. The trek takes around five hours and finishes at the village of **Káto Zákros** on the coast. Here you'll find several excellent tavernas on the water's edge and a flock of ducks eager to sample your leftovers.

The **Minoan Palace of Zákros** (open daily 8am–7pm) lies just behind this strand on flat ground, with its associated town rising up the hillside beyond. Zákros was well-situated for trade with Egypt and Syria to the east and it had a large port serving both commercial and naval vessels. The city was founded by the Minoans, as there are no earlier remains below the palace complex. Building began c.1900 BC, with remains from that date seen around the east wing. The palace proper was completed c.1600 BC, and the destruction of 1450 BC saw a complete collapse of the city; it was never resettled.

The **west wing** of the palace was given over to cult practices, with shrine, purification and libation rooms as in other Minoan sites, and workshops in the south. The **northern wing** housed the royal entourage and the main kitchen, while the east was reserved for the royal apartments. Many of these rooms had treasures in situ.

One unique aspect of Zákros is the water feature found in the east wing behind the royal apartments. The **cistern hall** contains a circular cistern, which is still full of water and now inhabited by a population of turtles. Nearby is a **ceremonial spring chamber** which has steps leading to a small,

Zákros, the last Minoan settlement to be excavated (in the 1960s), revealed a wealth of undisturbed artifacts. Tools and ceremonial objects were found just where they were dropped at the time of the great cataclysm, along with the crystal *rhyton* on view in the Iráklio Museum and a chest containing hundreds of clay tablets inscribed with Linear A script. Archaeologists even discovered an urn with olives preserved though the millennia.

square pool. You can then follow the traces of the paved road leading from the city to the ancient harbour, now lost beneath the waves.

The Southeastern Coast

Just beyond Gourniá it is possible to head south across the narrowest point on Crete to the coastal town of Ierápetra 14km (9 miles) away. However, if you have the time it is much more rewarding to do the circular journey along the north coast to Sitía then south around the Sitía and Ornón Mountain ranges approaching Ierápetra from the east – the landscape is more exciting and dramatic.

The mosque in Ierápetra, Europe's southernmost town

Ierápetra is the fourth-largest settlement on Crete and has the honour of being the southernmost town in Europe. It was the last Cretan city to fall to the Romans, who used it as a base for their conquest of Egypt. Today Ierápetra is a burgeoning resort, though it is much more laid back than those on the northern coast, making the most of its somewhat faded architecture, including a Venetian castle and a dilapidated mosque. What the town lacks in polish it makes up for in character – come here for genuine Cretan urban atmosphere. From the harbour you can also take trips to the southern island of **Hrýsí**. Only 13km (8 miles) from its larger sibling, Hrýsí still has unspoilt pine forest and pristine beaches to explore.

To the east and west of Ierápetra are tiny coastal settlements. Explore the Minoan settlements at **Pýrgos** and **Mýrtos** to the west or have a relaxed lunch at Mýrtos village or nearby **Tértsa**.

WESTERN CRETE

Western Crete offers a diverse range of attractions. Two delightful coastal towns on the north coast, unspoiled mountains where you can get back to nature or experience Cretan rural life, and tiny south-coast villages reached only on foot or by boat. Because of its mountains, this area is less densely populated than the east and has more rainfall, making it greener and much more lush. These contrasts make it a fascinating part of the island to spend a vacation.

Réthymno

The town of **Réthymno** lies 75km (50 miles) west of Iráklio, one hour away along the New National road. The site has been settled since Minoan times, with the remains of a Dorian, Greek and Roman town underlying the present buildings. Venetian rule spawned many of the architectural gems here, although evidence of Turkish rule can still be seen. Réthymno suffered many attacks and sackings over the centuries. Much of the town was badly damaged in the battle for Crete during World War II, although the heart of the Old Town survived. Today, a modern tourist sprawl has grown up to the east, taking advantage of the long sandy bay, but this has not spoilt the town itself – it's a delightful place in which to stroll. Take time to savour its Cretan atmosphere.

Réthymno has also been the intellectual centre of Crete throughout the ages and still contains a School of Philosophy.

In August each year the town draws intellectuals and artists from across Greece for its Renaissance Festival.

The Old Town occupies a strategic position on a nub of land jutting out from the long, flat coastline. A huge fortress – **the Fortezza** – dominates the site, its walls rising high above the streets on the northwestern point. This is thought to be the largest fortification ever built by the Venetians, who completed the task in 1586. The finest views of the walls are from the promenade on the waterfront, and as you walk you can truly appreciate its grand scale.

Once inside, it is easy to imagine a large garrison and its entourage being based here, although there are few buildings left to explore. There is, however, a small, whitewashed Orthodox chapel and the remains of barracks and arsenals. Ottoman forces made surprisingly light work of taking the fortress in 1646. They worshipped in a large mosque in

The Fortezza is the largest fortification the Venetians ever built

the centre of the fortress, whose interior you can explore. Perhaps the most exciting part of the tour is the view over Réthymno's Old Town from the parapets on the eastern side – myriad tiled rooftops lead down to the harbour beyond. There are also views east and west along the bay.

Immediately outside the entrance to the fortress is an old Ottoman garrison building now housing the **Archaeological Museum of Réthymno** (open Tues–Sun 8.30am–3pm). The collection covers finds from the Neolithic age onward and concentrates on Minoan finds in the 'lesser' sites (if one can use such a phrase for finds of this quality), as there are no major palaces in the area. Cave sites have rendered some particularly interesting votive artifacts. Excavations of tombs have also been fruitful and the museum displays some beautiful clay sarcophagi.

Walking right from the museum and right again along the waterfront brings you to the enchanting **Venetian inner harbour**, now a haven for small fishing craft and tour boats. At the end of the stone jetty is a lighthouse erected during Turkish rule, and the harbour cafés were where Ottomans used to socialise over dark, thick coffee and communal *nargilés* (hubble-bubble pipes). Nowadays, you can spend time here over a drink or an excellent fish dinner.

The maze of narrow streets behind the old harbour forms the core of the Old Town. Most are reserved for pedestrians only, inviting you to take an exploratory stroll. At every turn there is something to see; most obvious will be the wealth of shopping opportunities at eye level. Craft and jewellery stores create tempting displays, and cotton clothing is swathed across every wall.

However, don't neglect to look behind the wares to see Venetian stone lintels above, or to catch sight of ornate Otto-man balconies and pretty, wooden window frames dressed with bougainvillaea or honeysuckle. At night the streets here

Venetian and Turkish architecture combine in Réthymno's streets

come alive with shoppers and revellers, and there are excellent restaurants in some of the old buildings.

If you exit the harbour from the southwest you can cross busy Odós Arkadíou to traffic-free Odós Petiháki. On your left is the **Venetian Loggia**, built in 1600. Until recently it was sadly neglected but it has risen like a phoenix from the ashes and now performs the role of an up-market gallery where you can buy excellent copies of museum pieces. Walk down Petiháki to find the **Rimondi Fountain**. Built in the 1620s its once fine carvings have taken on an aged patina and it looks strangely out of place among the bright Internet cafés now replacing traditional tavernas in this bustling square.

From here the main shopping street, Odós Ethnikís Antistáseos, leads southwest. Turn right at Odós Vernárdou where you will find the **Nerantzés Mosque** (Djamí ton Nerantzión), now used as a concert hall. Beyond this is the **Historical Folk and Art Museum** (open Mon–Sat 10am–2pm), providing an evocative glimpse of the Crete of yesteryear. Everyday objects have been collected from households around the island, and these include clothing, domestic and farm tools, and samples of traditional crafts. Ponder over old photographs of Cretans in traditional costume and try to imagine just what the island must have been like during their lifetimes.

Continue along Ethnikís Antistáseos and you will reach the Venetian **Porta Goura Gateway** after a few minutes. This stone arch, once part of a greater structure, marks the boundary of

> Alise Rimondi, the Venetian commander, gave his name to the Rimondi Fountain. It is sometimes spelt 'Arimondi' – after someone mistakenly added his initial to his surname.

the Old Town, and beyond it you are immediately plunged into the traffic-filled world of the 21st century. Across this busy highway is the tempting shade of the **municipal gardens**, which host the wine festival each July.

Alternatively you could stroll along the waterfront east of the Venetian harbour. There's a good beach, and the town side of the street is lined with cafés and tavernas offering tourist menus. When you reach tiny Platía Iróon look for the minaret of **Kara Pasha Mosque** standing sentinel above the surrounding buildings.

South of Réthymno

The area south of Réthymno is well worth exploring by car to fully appreciate the rural lifestyle, but its major attraction can be visited by tour bus. **Arkádi Monastery** (Moní Arkadíou; open daily 8am–1pm, 3.30–8pm) lies in the foothills of the western Ida Mountains some 23km (14 miles) southeast of Réthymno. It was founded in the Byzantine era, although its present buildings date from the late 16th century, and is revered by Cretans as one of the centres of insurrection during the long struggle for independence.

In 1866 the islanders rose up once again to wrest control of their land from the Turks. As the bid failed, hundreds of partisans and their families sought sanctuary in the compound.

The Turks demanded their surrender and, when Abbot Gabriel (Gavriíl) refused, they attacked the monastery.

On 9 November the Turks broke through the outer walls to find the Greeks blockaded into a wine store-room, where they had a store of gunpowder. As Ottoman forces made their way toward this last refuge, the abbot ordered that a shot be fired into the explosive. The resulting blast killed hundreds of Cretans and Turks, giving real meaning to the battle cry of Crete – 'freedom or death'.

The tranquil cloisters of Arkádi, a monastery with a grim history

Today, the monastery is a much more peaceful place, although the wine storeroom remains a charred shell. The compound buildings have walls decorated with photographs and paintings of abbots and partisans; one room has a battle-plan relief map of the 1866 incident. The church that graces the middle of the compound is one of the most beautiful on Crete. Its façade of yellow sandstone is richly carved with a fine belltower, and mock Corinthian columns dignify each of the twin entranceways. Inside are fine icons, copies of which can be bought in the gift shop in the museum. This displays sacred vestments and some of the monastery's most valuable treasures.

Make your way back to the coastal road via **Elévtherna**, site of an ancient Doric site that has contributed artifacts to the archaeological collection at Réthymno, and **Margarítes**, a potter's village where you will be able to watch the artisans in action and buy some pretty souvenirs.

Directly south of Réthymno are two valleys leading to the south coast. The **Amári Valley** is the more easterly and the more exciting, with traditional rural landscapes to explore and dramatic views of Mount Ida (Psilorítis) as a backdrop. As you travel along you're sure to meet up with a shepherd herding his flock, or donkeys at the roadside taking a rest from the day's labours. The winding road leads through small villages, many graced with fine old churches.

At **Thrónos** visit the 14th-century **Panagía chapel** for its frescoes and the remains of an early Byzantine mosaic floor from a previous basilica – if the church is locked, ask at the shop next door as they keep a key. Head up the hill above the town to explore the remains of the ancient Greek town of **Syvritos**. **Asomáton** has a **Venetian monastery** now used as an agricultural college, and in **Monastiráki** there is a tiny Venetian chapel. The 'capital' of the region, the village of **Amári**, is worth taking time to explore. Its narrow, steep streets are waiting to reveal many secrets. The village's **Agía Ánna chapel** has the oldest frescoes on Crete, dating from 1225.

Margarítes is a good place to buy locally made pottery

The South Coast

The second valley to the west leads down to the agricultural centre of **Spíli**. Stop to try the waters at the **Venetian fountain** – a series of lion heads spout crystal clear, cool liquid from the

mountains above – before exploring the village itself. Although the main square does cater to visitors, the streets above have changed little over the generations.

Just before Spíli are roads leading right toward the coast and Moní Préveli (Préveli Monastery). The furthest north of these takes you through the dramatic **Kourtaliótiko Gorge**.

Moní Préveli (open daily 9am–1pm, 5–7pm) is a remote religious community and, like other such communities, was involved in partisan activities during Crete's struggles for freedom. An earlier monastery (Káto Préveli – you pass the evocative ruins on your way to the present-day site) was sacked by the Turks in 1821, and the fathers aided many Allied prisoners to escape in World War II. Préveli dates from the 16th century and was the richest religious order in Crete during the Ottoman era. Its treasures are on display in the museum shop. Do visit the church to see its splendid iconostasis, considered the best on the island. You'll also find a gold and diamond crucifix said to contain a piece of the True Cross.

From the monastery make your way along the south-coast road – a couple of kilometres (1 mile) inland – for an interesting tour. Nearby **Plakiás** is a burgeoning resort situated along a crescent-shaped bay. It makes a good base for a relaxing, low-key vacation. Further west, the walls of **Frangokástello** can be seen rising up above a sandy beach. This

Mists or Mysteries?

Every year in May local people living near Frangokástello say that they can see the spirits of the dead marching around the base of the castle. These *drosoulítes* or 'dewy ones' rise from the morning mists, and meteorologists assure us that they are simply a form of weather phenomena, not the spirits of the dead.

absolutely immense 14th-century fortress is now just an empty shell – like a set for a film about the French Foreign Legion. It was built not only to ward off pirate raids but also to prove Venetian might to the Cretan fighters in the mountains behind. During Turkish rule the fortress was the scene of many bloody events, including the capture of Daskalogiánnis in 1770 and the massacre of 700 Cretans in 1828. Statues nearby commemorate those who gave their lives.

If you want to take time for lunch make a point of stopping at **Hóra Sfakión**, as there are several good

Plakiás, a former fishing village, is a growing resort

tavernas along the waterfront of this small village. You'll also find a memorial to allied soldiers of World War II here, as the port was an evacuation point after the Battle of Crete in 1941. It is not possible to travel further west by road because the looming **White Mountains** (Lefká Óri) meet the sea here. Boats pick hikers up from the base of the Samariá Gorge, and at busy times rows of tour buses await their return. You can take boat trips to the island of **Gávdos**, the most southern territory in Europe, and to **Loutró**, a picturesque village with no vehicular access; or head inland on foot for Loutró and the remains of ancient **Anópoli** for an enjoyable day's hiking.

The traditional headwear of the fighting men of Sfakiá

Heading north by road once more, your journey will take you through the spectacular **Ímbros Gorge**, with its rich variety of flora and fauna – including, if you are lucky, the rare lammergeier or bearded vulture. This gorge is more accessible than nearby Samaria, and you can walk down through it by leaving your car at the village of Ímbros or up from Hóra Sfakión as the gradient is not too steep (8km/5 miles).

Réthymno to Haniá

The stretch of coastline between Réthymno and Haniá is developing fast. There are a number of new hotels at **Georgioúpoli,** a resort with a long, sandy beach and freshwater marshland on its western edge. **Kalýves** is also a lively resort village not yet swamped by tourism. The road leads on to **Soúda Bay**, home of Crete's largest port and one of the best deepwater anchorages in the Mediterranean. The Greek Navy has a large base here but the port also has a regular passenger and car ferry service to Piraeus near Athens. The west of the island was the initial landing spot for German forces in World War II and saw much fighting. The **British Commonwealth War cemetery** can be found at the head of the bay.

The **Akrotíri Peninsula** sits north of Soúda. Here you'll find Haniá's airport, several small villages and three important monasteries. Seventeenth-century **Agía Triáda** is still a major pilgrimage site and its church is decorated with impressive modern icons. **Moní Gouvernétou**, a smaller community, lies further north. Its icon of St John is the focus of many pleas for help. From here you can hike cross-country to the evocative remains of **Katholikó**, Crete's first monastery, founded in the 11th century by St John the Hermit. Set on the side of a rocky ravine and incorporating several caves, the monastery was sacked by pirates, after which the community moved to higher ground and founded Gouvernétou. As you head back toward Haniá stop at the **tomb of Elevthérios Venizélos** (1834–1936), Crete's greatest statesman, and that of his son. On this spot, on the orders of Venizélos, the Greek flag was raised in defiance of talks taking place among the major European powers about the fate of Crete. There are wonderful views across the bay to Haniá from here.

Haniá

The capital of Crete from 1845 until 1971, **Haniá** remains the island's second-largest settlement, notable for its extensive urban development. However, at its heart is the delightful Old Town replete with Venetian and Ottoman buildings and full of cosmopolitan atmosphere, considered to be one of the most beautiful towns in the whole of Greece.

The Old Town was once enclosed by high curtain walls; though today only the western curtain and **Shiavo-Lando Bastion** survive. It is well worth walking down Odós Pireós to examine the wall from beyond the protective ditch, to gain an impression of how the city used to look.

The **Venetian harbour** draws visitors and locals alike. It is huge by comparison with Réthymno and has an outer and inner section. The harbourfront is lined with beautiful medieval buildings and numerous cafés and tavernas, making it *the* place for the evening *volta* or stroll. The faded stucco of the harbour buildings takes on a delicate rosy hue as night falls, contrasting with the deep blue sky.

On the northwest corner of the outer harbour is **Firkás Tower**, a restored section of the Venetian ramparts housing the **Naval Museum** (Naftikó Mousío; open daily 10am–4pm), which displays fine model ships, maps and naval paraphernalia. Walk through the archway beyond the museum entrance for views east across the harbour from the tower walls. You'll see the impressive rounded dome of the **Mosque of the Janissaries** (Djamí ton Genissarión), built in 1645 and now an exhibition gallery, from where you can take a horse-and-carriage ride through the streets of the Old Town. Strolling past the mosque leads to the inner harbour, with the remains of large Venetian *arsenáli* (ship repair yards) – originally 17 lined the water's edge. You can then continue out along the pier to the lighthouse.

Tavernas line Haniá's attractive Venetian harbour

The Old Town fans out behind the harbour: narrow alleyways with a mélange of Venetian and Ottoman buildings, a canvas of faded terracotta and ochre stucco dressed with restaurant signs or wares for sale. The shopping here is the most sophisticated on Crete, a legacy of Haniá's days as an artistic hideaway in the 1960s. A pre-planned itiner-

Knitting in a Haniá courtyard

ary is not essential – you'll probably be drawn by a pretty-looking balcony, turn down an alleyway to watch kittens playing, then a boutique will catch your eye until eventually you've lost your bearings. That's all part of the appeal here, so relax and enjoy.

Although the streets all seem to run together, there are four sections of the Old Town. **Topanás**, behind the Naval Museum, was the Turkish administrative quarter – also where they kept their cannon. Odós Theotokopoúlou forms the uppermost street here, lined with fine Venetian mansions. Walk on to Odós Zambelioú to view the **Renieri Gate**, which was built in 1608.

Evraikí, to the southeast, was the Jewish Quarter during Venetian times. Its small houses awash with pastel hues form the core of shopping and eating possibilities. **Kastélli**, east of the Mosque of the Janissaries, was the centre of the Venetian city – as the name suggests there was an older castle here, rendered obsolete when the city expanded in the 16th century. You'll see remnants of the stone block walls and a Venetian arcade at the bottom of Odós Ágiou Márkou. This was also the site of Minoan, Greek and Roman Haniá called

Venetian streets in the Old Town

Kydonia. Scant remains of the Minoan city can be seen on Odós Karneváro. The easternmost section of the Old Town is **Splánzia**, characterised by cobbled alleyways and whitewashed churches. Platía 1821 forms the core of this quarter, which has more authentic Greek life than any other part of old Haniá.

Odós Halidón is a major thoroughfare that cuts the Old Town from the north to the south. Here, you will find Haniá's **Archaeological Museum** (open Tues–Sun 8.30am–3pm), housed within an old Venetian monastery. There are artifacts found at the Kydonia Minoan site, but equally impressive are Greco-Roman remains including a collection of Hellenistic mosaics.

Higher up Halidón, on the same side as the Archaeological Museum, is the **Cretan Folklore Museum** (open Mon–Sat 9am–3pm, 5–8pm), tucked away in a tiny square alongside the Roman Catholic cathedral. Walk down **Odós Skrydlóf** (Leather Street), with its bazaar-like atmosphere, to reach the **Agorá** covered market, one of the shopping highlights of Crete. Erected in 1911, its cross-shaped arcades offer cooling shade, and you can buy the best of the island's natural products as souvenirs, while locals shop for the night's meal. Look for the dried herb dittany *(díktamos)*, which is commonly used to make herbal tea.

West of Haniá

As there are no beaches near the town, the majority of people stay in resorts situated west of Haniá and simply travel in for the day. **Plataniás** is an excellent option with a lively atmosphere of its own, as is **Agía Marína**.

Further west the island takes on less of a tourist feel and agriculture becomes the main focus. **Máleme** is the furthest resort proper; after this, accommodation can be found only in private rooms or small local hotels. The town has a sad legacy, as it was at the airfield here that German paratroopers landed in 1941, signalling the start of the battle for Crete. Casualties were high for these pioneers, and the **German war cemetery** above the airfield holds the graves of more than 4,000 young men.

However, what this part of the island lacks in tourist facilities it more than makes up for in terms of open space and fresh air. Take to the hills along the rugged peninsulas of **Rodopoú** and **Gramvoúsa**, jutting out from the northern coast; or visit numerous small villages in the western foothills of the White Mountains. In the extreme far west, the wide sand beach at **Falássarna** attracts a lot of day-trippers from Haniá and further east.

The two islands off Gramvoúsa Peninsula both take its name – Iméri (tame) and Ágria (wild) Gramvoúsa.

The long road from Máleme to Paleohóra on the south coast could perhaps be said to provide a microcosm of what western Crete is all about. A wide, lush coastal plain fills the start of the journey, before the road climbs into the hills, which offer magnificent views to the east. As the road begins to drop from its apex, mountain villages sit astride it like jewels on a thread until you reach the coast. **Paleóhora** awaits, with a great range of eateries to replenish you for the journey home.

The White Mountains and the Samariá Gorge

The **White Mountains** (Lefká Óri) dominate the western part of the island. The highest range on Crete, with several of its peaks breaking 2,000m (5600ft), there are no villages in its shadow because the mountains rise steeply with no perceptible foothills. This is an untamed landscape, rugged and stunningly beautiful, with narrow valleys incised between limestone peaks that wear a mantle of snow until the early summer months. Yet in spite of this the mountains host one of Crete's most impressive, popular and enjoyable excursions – the 16-km (10-mile) walk down the famous **Samariá Gorge**.

The gorge is the longest in Europe and starts in the heart of the mountains at a mighty 3,352m (11,000ft). In winter its path carries melted water from the peaks above. Only in the mild conditions of summer, when the torrent turns to a trickle, are people allowed to follow its path. The journey brings home the true power and wonder of nature. High walls of stone, ancient cypress trees, rare orchids, and soaring birds of prey can all be seen.

Despite the strenuous nature of the trek – don't set out without sturdy footwear, a hat, sunscreen and an adequate supply of water – you'll share the narrow pathway with hundreds of other intrepid tourists, which adds to the camaraderie but can spoil the atmosphere if you wanted to be alone with nature. Try to make an early start if you can, say by 7am. Most people pay for an excursion that provides a bus ride to the head of the gorge at **Omalós** and boat transfer at

> **The Samariá Gorge is one of the few places where you might catch a glimpse of the elusive Cretan wild goat known as the *agrími* or *krí-krí*. Built like an ibex, with long curving horns, it is sometimes spotted leaping between crags in the White Mountains.**

the southern end, Agía Rouméli either east to Hóra Sfakión or west to Soúgia or Paleohóra where you rejoin the bus. If you travel independently you can take a bus from Haniá to Omalós and public transport from Hóra Sfakión back to Haniá, but confirm the timetables before you depart to avoid getting stranded. The gorge is open from 6am until sunset.

Park wardens give you a ticket, to be surrendered at the other end to ensure that no one is left stranded in the gorge at the end of the day, and the descent begins at the **xilóskalo** (wooden staircase), in fact a steeply descending path with wooden balustrades for much of the way.

Single file down the Samariá Gorge

With the wall of **Mt Gíngilos** towering above, the stone path drops sharply away in a series of switchbacks, falling 1,000m (3,300ft) in the first 3km (2 miles). Slippery scree slopes fall below, so take it easy and keep to the path.

The route becomes less steep once you reach the rest point at the **Chapel of Ágios Nikólaos**, 4km (2½ miles) in, where there is a picnic area. The freshwater pools are inviting, but swimming is strictly forbidden. The abandoned village of **Samariá**, with its 14th-century **Church of Osía María** (Mary's Bones), marks the halfway point. People lived here until 1962; now there's only a warden's post and first-aid station. Beyond is the gorge's narrowest point, the **Sideróportes**

Mount Gíngilos towers over the Samariá Gorge

(Iron Gates), only 3.5m (11ft) wide but 300m (1,000ft) high, a truly humbling sight and the most memorable, for from here the gorge opens up as it approaches the sea and is much less striking. The final stretch is perhaps the most gruelling as you walk along the shadeless riverbed, but at **Agía Rouméli** you'll be able to enjoy an extremely welcome drink.

EXCURSION TO SANTORÍNI

Although Crete is an interesting and varied island you may want to spend a day or two exploring a different Greek island. You can get to **Santoríni** to the north via a daily catamaran or weekly ferry from Iráklio, and this tiny rock in the Aegean makes an interesting contrast to its larger cousin.

The island of Santoríni (also called **Thíra**) is one of the most beautiful places in the world. Arriving by sea brings the stunning vista slowly into view allowing the full magnitude of its structure to open out in front of you, for Santoríni frames the largest volcanic crater on earth. A massive eruption of its volcano around 1500 BC carried the whole interior of the island high into the atmosphere, changing the climate of the earth for years afterwards. In place of land came water, surging in to fill the 11-km (7-mile) long void and causing massive tidal waves around the Mediterranean Sea.

What remains today is the outer rim of the original circular island. Sheer cliffs up to 300m (984ft) high bound the caldera, and a number of whitewashed settlements nestle along their crests – looking from a distance like icing melting down the sides of a Christmas cake.

Firá

The main town of the island is **Firá**, set on top of the high cliffs in the centre of the long interior curve. Its buildings tumble down towards the water below giving stunning views. A narrow, cobbled trail of 587 steps leads from the town to the small port below, now the domain of a fleet of donkeys that wait to carry cruise-ship passengers into town. For those wanting a quicker method, there is also a cable car that whisks you up from sea level in a couple of minutes. Most commercial ferries arrive at the new port of **Athiniás** further along the coast.

Firá is a shopper's paradise, a series of narrow alleys where you can wander free from the fear of traffic, although do keep eyes and ears open for donkeys. You can buy anything from a reproduction icon to a genuine Fabergé egg, designer jewellery of the finest quality and designer clothing by the most desirable names. Find a spot for a drink at sunset, which has to be one of the most spectacular on earth.

Among the boutiques and bars are two places of cultural interest: the **Archaeological Museum** (open Tues–Sun 8.30am–3pm), with pottery and other artifacts found on the island, and the **Mégaron Gýzi Museum** (open daily May–Sept 10.30am–1.30pm, 5–8pm) north of the cable-car station, which is housed in a beautiful 17th-century fortified house. Most exciting of its varied collections is a display of photographs showing island scenes from before the devastating 1956 earthquake – the last major one to strike the island.

Ía

Firá is beautiful but can get a little oppressive, as visitors crowd the narrow streets. A little way north is a smaller town where the pace is a little less frantic. **Ía** (pronounced Oia), set on the northern cliffs, became home to a number of artists and still maintains a more bohemian atmosphere than Firá. There are many homes built into the hillsides, and some have been converted into art galleries and shops selling crafts and souvenirs. Its typical Cycladic architecture and multicoloured façades make it one of the most photographed villages in the world.

Whitewashed Ía is sprinkled with blue-domed churches

Pýrgos and Akrotíri

Aside from the stunning views, Santoríni has many more delights to show its visitors, with 12 villages to visit set among agricultural land. The fertile volcanic soil is blanketed in vines or in plants producing tiny sweet tomatoes. In the centre of the island is the village of **Pýrgos**, with the remains of a Venetian fortress at its heart. On a rocky bluff beyond the village you will find the 17th-century **Monastery of Profítis Ilías**. The monastery is only open when the priests inside take liturgies – mornings or early evenings – but it is well worth taking the time to visit. Pride of place goes to a 15-century icon of the prophet Elijah. It also has a museum, which conveys a flavour of monastic life, with icons and manuscripts. Unfortunately, the hilltop is also shared with the Greek military and it bristles with satellite and digital technology, prohibiting photography of the beautiful panorama. On the east coast are beaches of fine black or red sand – another legacy of the volcanic activity – which heat to a ferocious temperature in the summer sun.

In the south of the island is one of the most important ancient sites in the Mediterranean. Near the modern village of **Akrotíri**, a complete city was discovered dating from before 2000 BC. It was totally covered by several feet of ash during the eruption c.1500 BC but, unlike the tragic city of Pompeii in Italy, no human remains have been found, leading scientists to believe that the population escaped before the disaster took place. Since 1967 the site has been painstakingly excavated to give a picture of daily life before the great eruption. A society of complexity and sophistication is being unveiled, including organised urban planning, heating, sanitation and a standard script. However, much of the beautiful artwork found here is, for the moment, in the Archaeological Museum in Athens. The remains, including streets with houses and communal squares, have been placed under a protective corrugated roof that gets hot and crowded, so visit as early in the day as possible.

WHAT TO DO

SPORTS

Beach Activities

Crete has hundreds of beaches, from tiny coves to lengthy strands. You can choose to spend your day with hundreds of other people, or have the sand all to yourself at a remote spot. Beaches in the main resorts have well-organised watersports facilities with jet-skis and water rides, kayaking and parasailing. The best are at Ágios Nikólaos, Hersónisou, Mália, Agía Pelagía and Réthymno on the north coast.

South-coast resorts tend to be more low-key than their northern counterparts. Beaches are generally smaller, in bays rather than in long stretches of shoreline. You'll find the most diverse range of beach activities at Mátala, Agía Galíni, Plakiás and Elavónisos.

Vái, in the far northeastern corner, is considered the best beach on the island, and for this reason it gets busy in summer. Most of the out-of-the-way beaches, where you can find some solitude, are at the end of tortuous lanes in remote parts of the island. Try Xerókambos south of Zákros, or head east from Moní Préveli to the sandy stretches around tiny Agía Fotiní.

Walking and Hiking

This is an ideal island for taking to the countryside. You will be well rewarded on a walk, with small remote villages, hidden churches and a rural lifestyle to explore. Although Cretans are bemused as to why anyone would want to hike without any purpose but for the pleasure of it, they have a genuine welcome for travellers on foot. Itineraries can range from short easy walks to steep mountain hikes; however, it's not advisable to head into the high peaks without a guide.

Rugged walking country: the Valley of the Dead

Gorge walks are particularly popular; the Samariá is the busiest and the longest. Others include the Ímbros Gorge near Samariá, and the Valley of the Dead at Zákros on the east coast. The peninsulas off the northwest coast present dramatic and interesting walks. Akrotíri is the most populated, and not as rugged as Gramvoúsa and Rodopoú, which are wild and windswept. Shorter itineraries could include the walk from Ágii Déka to Gortys; from Mália to the Minoan site to the east; or from village to village in the Amári Valley.

Diexodos (tel/fax: 28410 28098) is a well-established company that organises guided hiking tours either by the day or longer. They can supply equipment and extra insurance if you need it.

Cycling

Many of these same itineraries can be covered on two wheels as well as on two feet, and mountain biking and bicycle touring are becoming increasingly popular. Once in the hinterland, however, you will need stamina to make it up the hills and mountain passes. Diexodos *(see details above)* also organises bike tours, or you can rent equipment in all the major resorts and plan your own itinerary.

Diving and Snorkelling

The waters around the island offer interesting diving and snorkelling opportunities for water-lovers with all levels of experience. Although the Mediterranean is overfished, and the waters are not warm enough to support colourful tropical fish, there are still numerous varieties to spot in the rocky shallows, including octopus that make their homes in crevices.

The remains of many ancient sites lie just off the coast. At Eloúnda you can explore the remains of Oloús, and Mátala has a port and harbour pier. The Greek government is concerned that archaeological treasures do not disappear and for this reason diving is allowed only with a qualified dive company that will oversee underwater locations and activities.

If you have never tried scuba-diving before, each dive centre is registered by the Greek government to offer training in addition to dive supervision for qualified divers. The basic qualification, the Open Water Certificate, takes five days to complete. Many centres also offer an introductory session commonly known as the Discover SCUBA Programme.

> **If you are learning to dive for the first time, make sure that you choose a dive centre that is affiliated with one of the major certifying bodies: PADI (the Professional Association of Diving Instructors) is the most common.**

ENTERTAINMENT

A huge number of fairs and festivals take place throughout the year. Your local tourist office will have details of what's taking place during your stay on Crete. Each community celebrates its own Saint's Day, when the sacred statue is paraded through the streets. After a solemn religious service, the rest of the day is given over to revelry. These are the best places to see traditional Cretan dances and live music, and to join in with local people having some fun. Each village has one at some time during the year, so there's sure to be an opportunity to take part.

Music and Dance

For many, the image of Greek music and dance is inexorably linked to the film *Zorba the Greek*. Anthony Quinn performs the *syrtáki* dance (an amalgam of several traditional dances) to the sound of the *bouzoúki*, a stringed mandolin-type instrument that produces melodic, slightly metallic sounds. When played live it has a haunting melody, but taverna owners do have the irritating habit of playing it at high decibels through overloaded speakers. This does a great disservice to the Greek musical tradition, which is rich, varied and ancient. The tradition is still particularly strong on Crete where classic musicians and singers are held in high regard.

Musical rhythms were traditionally matched to the complex cadences of the epic poetry of Greece. These are very

---

Zorba's Dance

The film *Zorba the Greek* brought international fame to author Níkos Kazantzákis. Michalis Cacoyannis, a Hollywood producer of Cypriot origin, made the film in 1964, with Anthony Quinn in the leading role as Zorba. The famous *syrtáki* dance caused a number of problems for the islanders as it is not a genuine Cretan dance at all. The real thing proved too difficult for the American actor to learn, so composer Theodorákis came up with a simple but haunting melody in its place. The hordes of tourists who later came to Crete asked to see a dance that did not actually exist, but hoteliers and the music industry moved quickly to fill the gap. *Syrtáki* is performed at today's 'Cretan evenings', and cassettes of the catchy tune are available everywhere.

different from the 'four beats to a bar' that characterises the western musical tradition, so it is sometimes difficult for Western listeners to follow. Songs have traditionally been sung by men – relating the hard life of the farmer or fisherman and including an element of sentimentality that is rarely expressed in other areas of a Greek male's life.

Crete's main traditional musical instrument is the *lýra*, a three-stringed fiddle, played upright. It is usually accompanied by the *laoúto*, a development of the Arab *oud* (lute); the *askomandoúra*, Cretan bagpipes; and the *habióli*, the shepherd's

Traditional costume is worn for performances of traditional music

flute. The instruments are brought together in *mantinádes* songs with rhyming couplets of lyrics. Many of these have been passed down through generations of Cretans. The fighters of the western mountains had their own songs, the *rizitiká*, with lyrics praising bravery and patriotism. The mountain men also have their own dances; Réthymno has its own dance, the *soústa,* with hopping steps.

Chanting epic poetry is also a Cretan tradition that has been carried through the generations. This would have strengthened the bonds of lonely, frightened young fighters and stirred their blood before action. The 17th-century *Erotókritos*, written by Vitséntzos Kornáros, is the most popular of these.

The town of Réthymno holds a number of festivals throughout the summer, with the municipal gardens and fortress the usual venues. The July Music Festival is followed by the Renaissance Festival in August. This includes numerous classical performances.

The larger hotels will usually hold a 'Greek' evening on one night each week. The music and dance is usually of a high standard, although the surroundings can be less than authentic. The settlement of Áno Hersónisou, known locally as Koutalafári, just inland from the resort, holds a weekly Greek evening in the village square. It's full of atmosphere, and there is a selection of tavernas where you can enjoy a meal while watching the show.

SHOPPING

Shopping is one of the delights of a trip to Crete; souvenirs abound in all ranges of price and quality. Most of the souvenir shops in the major resorts cater to the popular, but you don't need to look far to find locally produced goods that make wonderful mementoes of your trip, and the narrow streets of the old towns are places where you can browse for hours. Prices can be flexible, particularly in tourist shops and at the beginning and end of the season, so don't seem too eager to pay the marked price.

Textiles

Sheep's wool and goat's hair have always been used to produce material, clothing and interesting rugs, carpets and throws. You can still buy handmade pieces – *yfandá* – with traditional designs, or machine-produced items. Brighter colours often indicate synthetic dyes, whereas traditionally-made items are still made with the muted earthy colours of natural dyes. The price differential will also indicate the difference between the two. Dolphins and fish are popular themes, as are stylised images of Greek gods. You'll find particularly interesting ranges in Kritsá and Anógia, and also on the approach to the Dictaean Cave in Lassíthi and in shops in Haniá. The only remaining traditional loom weaver in Crete is Mihális Manousákis in Haniá.

If rugged textiles don't appeal, then you'll also find beautiful embroidered items such as cotton and linen tablecloths and napkins. Again the hand-embroidered pieces are the best and most expensive, but this skill is a dying art, so good examples will become harder to find. However, you will have

Souvenirs for sale outside the Mosque of the Janissaries, Haniá

plenty of everyday tablecloths to choose from in markets and the main tourist centres.

Leather Goods

Leather has been extremely good value in Greece for many years. Bags, purses, luggage and belts can be found in abundance – try Odós Skridlóf (Leather Street) in Haniá to begin comparing quality and prices.

The traditional leather sandals (flat soles with leather straps) are still sold in the streets of Réthymno and Haniá. There is also a workshop at Kritsá, but nowadays modern mass-produced fashion shoes seem to be invading the scene.

You can also purchase a pair of Cretan farmer's boots – almost knee-high black leather with thick leather soles. They are guaranteed to last a lifetime and, to judge by the number of well-worn pairs on feet in the hinterland, that certainly seems true. These are handmade and will take about a week to complete.

Hand-forged Cretan knives are made by experienced knife-maker Apostólos Pahtikoó, at his shop O Arménis ('the Armenian') located on Odós Sífaka in Haniá's Old Town. Watch him forge the blade and fit it to a wooden, bone or horn handle before putting a razor edge to the stainless-steel blades.

Clothing

In terms of fashions for the hot weather, you should easily be able to buy everything you need in Crete, so don't worry if you can't find the appropriate summer clothes or swimwear at home before you leave. Greek cotton is manufactured into a range of good-value, cool cotton clothing that is perfect for touring and exploring. Shorts, trousers, shirts and dresses are sold in shops and at stalls in all the major towns; it's just a matter of finding a style that

Leather goods galore in Haniá's Odós Skridlóf

you like. Early and late in the season you'll be able to buy good- quality cotton sweaters to guard against the evening chills. Cream and blue tend to be the most popular colours.

Stores in Iráklio stock all the major European designer street names along with many US labels. Prices are much the same as elsewhere in the European Union.

Edibles

Olives and olive oil are obvious choices to take home. The quality of both is excellent and considered among the best in Greece. Particularly good are the extra virgin cold-pressed oils from Sitía, Toploú and Agía Triáda.

Honey is also one of the prime staples of the Cretan diet. Wild herbs and flowers on the hills impart a wonderful flavour, and you can buy it plain or with nuts added.

A variety of herbs are collected and dried for you to take home and use in your cooking. Basil, thyme and oregano are the most common, though you can also

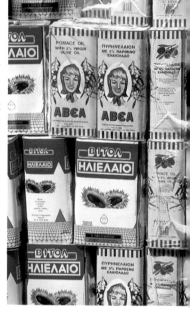

Olive oil and sunflower oil

buy mixed sachets. Dittany (*díktamos*) is a popular herb that is boiled to make tea.

Art and Icons

Artists flocked to Haniá in the 1960s and '70s, and this has left a legacy in the quality of work on sale here (and to a lesser extent across Crete). There are several galleries displaying work by local and international artists in the narrow alleyways of the Evraikí Quarter. A more Greek form of art is that of the icon. Icons are religious portraits, usually of a saint or apostle, and lie at the heart of Byzantine or Orthodox worship as they form a focus for prayer. The characteristic gold leaf used in their production symbolised the glory of God.

For centuries icons were popular souvenirs of the grand European Tour or religious pilgrimage. However, modern production methods, including thin artificial canvas and gaudy synthetic colours, saw them lose favour. In recent years there has been a rebirth in icon painting using traditional methods, both for church renovations and for commercial sale. This time-consuming work is exquisite and correspondingly expensive. Most monasteries on Crete create certified copies of their most celebrated icons, and you can also find them in jewellery shops and speciality stores in the towns.

Jewellery

Both gold and silver are sold by weight, with relatively little extra cost for workmanship, so they represent good value for money. Ancient Minoan patterns are common with necklaces, bracelets and rings in matching sets. You can also find items featuring precious and semi-precious stones.

There are some excellent copies of museum pieces for sale. These will come complete with a certificate of authentication, which you may need to show to customs as you depart. If you want to buy a genuine antique (anything produced before 1821), you will need a permit before you can export it. Always consult an expert when you do this in order to avoid subsequent problems.

However, you don't need a large budget to buy trinkets; popular street jewellery uses leather, semi-precious stones and crystals.

Pottery and Ceramics

It's not surprising – given the importance of pottery throughout Crete's history – that it is still a significant industry. Pieces come as small as a ring holder or olive bowl to huge garden pieces that would have to be shipped back home. Both unglazed and ceramic styles

Handmade knives and worry-beads for sale in Réthymno

are available; most notable of these is the bright-blue glaze of Haniá ceramics. Traditional designs abound, including marine themes, Minoan designs and Classical Greek imagery. Modern abstract pieces can also be found, particularly in Haniá, where there are galleries stocked by avant-garde potters. At Margarítes you can watch the potters at work and buy from their workshops.

CHILDREN'S CRETE

A visit to Crete isn't all about museums and ancient sites – there's also lots of fun to be had for younger members of the family. Greek society is very family-oriented, and children will be very welcome at tavernas and cafés.

Beach activities are well-organised on the northern coast, with all types of watersports and rides. The best sandy beaches are at Mália, Réthymno, Georgioúpoli and Vái, with organised activities at Agía Pelagía. South-coast resorts such as Plakiás and Mátala have good beaches and plenty of snorkelling opportunities for older children. Water-parks at Hersónisou and Mália will keep them occupied for hours. Don't forget that the sun can be very strong in summer, so always make sure that young skin is adequately protected, even when children are playing in the water.

At Greek evenings, hotels usually allow children to get up on the dance floor and try the steps for themselves.

A horse-and-carriage ride through the streets of Haniá is a great treat and gives young children a good vantage point. They can even sit next to the driver. Trips along the coast in colourful *caïques* offer the chance to enjoy a cooling breeze and an alternative view of the island. Castles such as Koúles in Iráklio and Frangokástello allow imaginations to run wild – Dad will believe he's Errol Flynn, and the children might choose to be Hercules or Xena.

Shopping is so varied that even the most meagre pocket-money should be able to fund a spending spree. The traffic-free streets in Réthymno and Haniá are a young shopper's paradise. At the other end of the scale, the rural lifestyle of the interior

Children might like to take a carriage ride in Haniá

will delight urban children – watching goat herds filing past or donkeys working hard for their owners. Somnolent cats and playful kittens abound, and sea ducks and geese can be found at many coastal fishing villages.

If you want to spend some time apart from your children, the majority of large hotels have good children's clubs, where the days will be filled with fun activities.

Calendar of Festivals

Crete has numerous festivals and celebrations throughout the year. Each community celebrates its own saint's day, and there are simply too many of these celebrations, called *panigýri*, to list here. Ask in your local tourist office about those taking place during your stay. Listed below are the major events taking place across the island.

1 January: St Basil's Day. Sprigs of basil offered as tokens of hospitality.

6 January: *Theofáni* (Epiphany). Youths dive for coins thrown into harbours.

February/March: Street carnivals in Réthymno and Iráklio during the two weeks before Lent, culminating in 'Clean Monday' – the first day of Lent when houses are spring-cleaned.

March/April: Easter. Candlelight processions on Good Friday; effigy of Judas burned on Saturday, with fireworks; in churches the sacred flame passes to a candle for each household; on Sunday a lamb is sacrificed. Flower festival held in Réthymno.

23 April: Ágios Geórgios (St George), patron saint of shepherds, is celebrated in many rural villages. Sheep-shearing festival in Así Goniá.

20–7 May: Battle of Crete commemorated in Máleme and Haniá. Music and dancing.

24 June: Ioánnis o Pródromos (St John the Baptist). Celebrated with bonfires in many parts of the island.

July: Marine week with celebrations at all the ports. Réthymno hosts a Wine Festival and a Music Festival.

August: Renaissance festival in Réthymno; wine festival in Sitía.

15 August: *Apokímisi tís Panagías* (Assumption of the Virgin). Celebrated throughout Crete, especially at monasteries dedicated to the Virgin.

25 August: Ágios Títos (St Titus, patron saint of the island). Large procession in Iráklio.

29 August: Ágios Ioánnis (John the Baptist). Pilgrimage to Ágios Ioánnis on the Rodopoú Peninsula and services at other churches dedicated to him.

28 October: *Ochi* Day. Celebrating Greek defiance in World War II.

7–9 November: Commemoration of the Arkádi Monastery explosion with a fireworks display.

EATING OUT

Greek food has always incorporated local and seasonal ingredients at the peak of their flavour and freshness, whether eaten raw or cooked in the simplest ways. Since the island was settled several millennia ago, the people of Crete have relied on staples such as excellent olive oil, fragrant wild herbs, seafood, lamb or goat meat, and an abundance of fresh vegetables, fruit, pulses and nuts. Put these together with more recent Venetian and Ottoman influences, and you have an interesting menu from which to choose. The island shares many recipes with its mainland countrymen, but it also has several ingredients and dishes found nowhere else in Greece.

Today, the traditional Cretan diet is considered to be one of the healthiest in the world, and it is well worth following the local people to the better eateries to try it. You may find yourself dining away from the pretty views, but you can be sure that the food will be excellent. Prices in all but the most luxurious establishments are government-controlled.

Where to Eat

Crete has a whole range of eateries specialising in certain types of food. Although the boundaries between them are blurring, here is an explanation of the types of traditional eateries you will find.

The *ouzerí* is a traditional establishment selling not only the fiery alcoholic drink after which it is named, but also the *mezédes* dishes that accompany it – ouzo is never drunk on an empty stomach. Octopus (or squid) is traditional but it is not compulsory.

The *kafeníon* is the Greek coffee shop, traditionally the domain of the male, and still so in the inland villages. Usually very plainly decorated, with a few old tables and chairs outside, it is the focus of heated political debate and serious backgammon games.

The *psistariá* offers food on-the-go. It serves *gýros* and *souvláki*, fast foods that make for a tasty lunch or snack. After your savoury courses, peruse the amazing choice at the *zaharoplastía* (pastry shop) or the *galaktopolío*, which specialises in yoghurt, cheese and other dairy dishes. However, the *tavérna* is at the heart of Greek hospitality, where appetiser and entrée courses are served. They are often family-run and offer a range of local dishes.

All restaurants will make a cover charge. This is usually no more than €1 per person

The *kafeníon* is the traditional rendez-vous for village men

and includes a serving of bread – if you can, try *paximádia* (the traditional Cretan heavy bread) or *dákos* (barley rusks).

When to Eat

Many tavernas in the major resorts open for breakfast, lunch and dinner. Breakfast has traditionally been a small meal for Greeks – Continental-style with bread, jam or honey and coffee. Lunch is eaten at around 3pm, followed by a siesta before work begins again at 5.30pm. Dinner is late, usually at around 10pm, although in summer, tavernas will serve food as late as 1am. If you want to eat early, most tavernas will begin their evening service at around 6pm.

WHAT TO EAT

In the majority of traditional restaurants you will be presented with an extensive menu; however, note that not everything on the menu is always available – many foods are seasonal or made in batches (such as *mousakás*). Items currently available will have a price in pencil beside them, although even this can be inaccurate, if the clientele has favoured one particular dish that day.

Some of the best and most authentic Cretan restaurants will not even have a menu. Here, you simply go into the kitchen or to the grill to see what looks and smells most enticing, then you simply make your choice.

Keftédes, tiropitákia, dolmádes and a Greek salad or *horiátiki*

Appetisers

Greece is one country where appetisers can constitute a full meal. *Mezédes* (a selection of small appetiser dishes) shared by the whole table, is a fun and relaxing way to eat. Tavernas have no qualms about taking orders for 'appetisers only' meals.

The most popular *mezédes* include *tzatzíki* (yoghurt flavoured with garlic, cucumber and mint); *dolmádes* (vine leaves stuffed with rice and vegetables – and sometimes with meat); olives; *taramá* (cod-roe paste blended with breadcrumbs, olive oil and lemon juice); *gí-gantes* (large beans in tomato sauce); *kalamári* (deep-fried squid); *pastourmá (*a kind of garlic sausage made with mutton or beef); and *keftédes (*small meatballs flavoured with coriander and spices). *Saganáki* is a slice of feta cheese coated in breadcrumbs and fried, but you can also have feta wrapped in foil with garlic and herbs and cooked in the oven. Cretan specialities include *tiropitákia* (pastry parcels filled with cheese) and *salingária* (snails).

Greek salad or *horiátiki* (literally 'village salad') of tomato, cucumber, onion and olives topped with feta, can be eaten as a meal by itself. When adding salad dressing, always add vinegar to the salad first followed by oil.

Soups are a staple of the diet in winter, but availability is more limited in summer. *Psarósoupa* (fish soup) is a standard on many seafood restaurant menus along with *kalamaráki* (squid). Cretan soups of *fakés* (lentil), *revíthia* (chickpea) or *fasólia* (bean) are excellent. *Avgolémono* (chicken broth with egg, lemon and rice), although delicious, is now harder to find.

Fish

It's no surprise that for centuries seafood formed a major part of the diet for islanders. You'll find the day's catch on ice outside a taverna and will be asked to make your choice, which will be weighed before cooking. Ask the price if you are on a budget, as seafood is always a relatively expensive option by Greek standards.

The most common types of fish are *barboúnia* (red mullet), *xifías* (swordfish), *glóssa* (sole) and *lithríni* (bream). Seafood is always best served simply and it is often grilled with fresh lemon. *Marídes* (little fish or whitebait) and *sardéles* (sardines) are served fried. If you like seafood stewed, try the *ktapódi* (octopus) with white wine, potatoes

An enticing display of fresh fish and seafood

and tomatoes; or *garídes* (prawns), which are typically served with a white-wine sauce or sauce mixed with feta cheese.

Meat

Fast foods to eat on the move include *souvláki* (small chunks of meat on a skewer also known internationally by the Turkish name *kebab*) or *gýros* (thin slices of meat cut from a spit and served with salad on pita bread, known to the Turks as *doner kebab*). More formal barbecued dishes may include whole chickens, sides of lamb and veal, or stuffed loin of pork, all cooked to melting perfection. *Brizóla* is a basic steak, and it may come well done rather than rare. Roasted or barbecued lamb is the traditional Easter fare.

Slow-cooked oven dishes and stews are worth trying. *Kléftiko* is braised lamb with tomatoes, while *stifádo* is braised beef with onions – each comes in a small earthenware pot that keeps the contents piping hot. In village tavernas you may still be able to find *katsíki* (goat in tomato sauce) or *loukánika* (sausages), particularly *kokorétsi* (sausage made of tripe and herbs).

Greece's most famous dish is probably *mousakás* – layers of aubergine (eggplant) and minced lamb with onions topped with a generous layer of béchamel sauce. At its best it should be firm but succulent and aromatic with herbs. The best restaurants will make a fresh batch daily. *Pastítsio* is another layered dish, this time of pasta (macaroni), meat and tomato sauce. *Giouvétsi* is beef stewed with lozenge-shaped pasta.

For those who want a hot vegetarian dish, *gemistá* consists of tomatoes, aubergine or peppers stuffed with a rice and vegetable mixture, or oven-cooked vegetables in a tomato sauce.

Cheeses

Most Greek and Cretan cheese is made from ewe's or goat's milk. The best-known soft cheese is *féta,* a main ingredient in Greek salads. *Kaséri,* a hard cheese, is nicest eaten fresh, but can also be grated, like Parmesan, and used in cooked dishes. Cretan cheeses include *anthótyro* and *manoúri,* both fairly mild. Harder, with more of a 'bite', are *agrafoú* and *kefalotíri.*

Dessert

Most tavernas will bring a plate of fresh fruit as a finale to your meal. If you feel the need for something more substantial, the

---

Snail Delicacies

Snails from Crete are much prized throughout Greece and are even exported to France. Although they are eaten throughout the year, snails are a Lenten speciality. They are prepared in a variety of ways: scalded in salted water; cooked with rice, tomatoes and garlic; cooked in *rakí;* or, best of all, fried with ground tomatoes, potatoes and thyme, in a dish called *egíni. Salingária stifádo* is snail stew.

Sticky sweet cakes for sale

zaharoplastío is the place to go. Here, perhaps, is the longest-lasting legacy of the Turks, who introduced a number of highly decadent sweets. You will find *baklavás*, layers of honey-soaked flaky pastry with walnuts; *kataïfi,* shredded wheat filled with chopped almonds and honey; *loukoúmi* a honey-flavoured fritter; or *pítta me méli*, honey cake.

If you prefer dairy desserts, try delicious Cretan yoghurt with local honey or fruit. *Rizógalo* is a kind of cold rice pudding, while *galaktoboúreki* is a type of custard pie.

WHAT TO DRINK

Cretan wine has been celebrated throughout history and only lost favour internationally in relatively modern times. Recent innovations are now improving the reputation of bottled wines, but they are expensive by the standards of other Greek wine.

Another option is to order wine from the barrel, whereby a basic 'village' wine – red/white/rosé – will be served young and cool. Crete excels in the production of such wine, and each region's production has its own flavour and colour. Wine of this type is usually very reasonably priced.

Greece also produces *retsína*, wine flavoured with resin – particularly useful in ancient times to keep the wine fresh in the hot climate. *Retsína* goes well with the Greek diet, or with a dash of soda water, but it is an acquired taste.

Oúzo is taken as an aperitif, neat, or with ice and water. The distilled alcohol, which is flavoured with aniseed, seems to cool the blood. The even stronger *rakí* is more popular among Cretans. This is the same alcohol but without the aniseed. Don't overdo either, as too much can pack a mighty hangover.

If you prefer beer you can find Amstel and Heineken, brewed under licence on the Greek mainland, but Mythos is a native Hellenic beer that has a very crisp taste.

Non-Alcoholic Drinks

The Greeks have fallen in love with the café frappé – strong, cold coffee served over ice. Hot coffee is *kafé ellinikó* or Greek style (indistinguishable from Turkish coffee), freshly brewed in individual copper pots and served in small cups. It will automatically arrive *glykó* (very sweet) unless you order *métrio* (medium) or *skéto* (without sugar). Italian *espresso* and *cappuccino* can be found in the upmarket cafés along the harbour-fronts and in Iráklio. Instant coffee is known by its trade name – Nescafé or *nes*. *Nes me gála* is instant coffee with milk.

Traditional food and drink – oúzo, wine, rakí and honey

Soft, fizzy drinks come in all varieties on Crete and you could also try one of the most refreshing drinks available – Cretan mineral water fresh from mountain springs.

Dittany (*díktamos*) is a herb sold across the island. It is used to make a herbal infusion that is believed to have beneficial effects on the digestion and other ailments. You won't find it on many restaurant menus but you may be offered it if invited to a Cretan home.

To Help you Order...

Could we have a table?	**Boroúme na éhoume éna trapézi?**
I'd like a/an/some...	**Tha íthela...**
The bill, please	**To logariasmó, parakaló**
napkin	**trapezomándilo**

one	**ena/mia**	three	**tris/tría**
two	**dío**	four	**tésera**

...and Read the Menu

aláti	salt	**melitzána**	aubergine
arní	lamb	**neró**	water
avgó	egg	**pagotó**	ice cream
barboúnia	red mullet	**pedákia**	lamb chops
elyés	olives	**pepóni**	melon
fasolákia	green beans	**pipéri**	pepper
gála	milk	**psári**	fish
garídes	prawns	**psitó**	grilled
gemistés	stuffed	**psomí**	bread
hirinó	pork	**revíthya**	chickpeas
hórta	boiled greens	**skórdo**	garlic
kalamarákia	squid	**spanakópita**	spinach pie
kotópoulo	chicken	**stafília**	grapes
kounéli	rabbit	**sto foúrno**	roasted
krasí	wine	**tyrópita**	cheese pie
kréas	meat	**vodinó**	beef
ktapódi	octopus	**voútyro**	butter
ládi	olive oil	**xifías**	swordfish

HANDY TRAVEL TIPS

An A–Z Summary of Practical Information

A

ACCOMMODATION (See also RECOMMENDED HOTELS, page 132)

Hotels: Many hotels in the resorts have contracts with tour operators. If you are travelling in July or August, always make a firm reservation before you arrive to avoid disappointment. In April and October prices are generally much lower than at peak season. Most tourist hotels close from November to March, although business hotels in the larger towns stay open all year.

Pensions: This is simple accommodation in small, usually family-run, establishments with no extra facilities such as a restaurant or bar, or reception services. Generally they are spotlessly clean and offer good value for those on a budget.

Private accommodation: Many families have rooms that they let to visitors; they will meet you at the ferry port with photographs of their accommodation. Most have simple furniture, a small kitchenette and basic bathroom facilities. It helps to know the geography of the island, as some private rooms can be some distance away from the main towns or resorts. Réthymno and Haniá offer better options than Iráklio if you want to stay in town.

I'd like a single/double room **Tha íthela éna monóklino/díklino**
   with bath/shower   **me bánio/dous**
What's the rate per night?   **Póso éki/stihízi gia káthe vrádi?**

AIRPORTS

The main airport (tel: 28102 28402) is situated 5km (3 miles) west of Iráklio. This serves regular traffic from Athens and numerous charter flights for central and eastern resorts. There is also an airport (tel: 28210 63245) at Haniá, taking flights from Athens and charter flights for the western part of the island. You can also fly from Athens, Thessaloniki, Prevéza and Alexandroúpoli to Sitiá, an airport (tel: 28430 22270) that is undergoing a massive expansion.

From all three airports there are taxis into town. Iráklio also has a bus service to and from Platía Elevtherías. Haniá's bus service takes you to the main bus station.

B

BICYCLE AND MOPED HIRE (RENTAL)

Bicycle hire: There are several companies that arrange bicycle tours where your luggage is transported to your next hotel while you travel in convoy with other cyclists. The mountain roads can be steep and long, and it's not a vacation to be undertaken lightly. The flat northern coastline is also suitable for cycle traffic, though your fellow road users are not always the best-mannered. Níkos on Odós Bofor in Iráklio (tel: 28102 26425) supplies advice and bikes.

Moped/scooter hire: Hiring a small motorbike is inexpensive – around €20 per day for a 50cc machine, less if you hire for three days or more. You should always wear a helmet on a scooter or moped (it is the law in Greece) and proceed with caution. It is illegal to ride a bike *with any size engine* without a motorcycle licence – but many hire agencies ignore this legislation. If you ride a motorbike without the right licence, any insurance you have will be void and could create grave difficulties if you are involved in an accident.

What's the hire charge for a full day?	**Póso kostízi giá mía méra?**

BUDGETING FOR YOUR TRIP

Crete offers excellent value for money, with hotel rooms and food prices controlled by the Greek government in most categories. Here are some approximate prices to help you to plan your budget.

Flight from Athens to Iráklio €75
Adult ferry ticket from Athens €30
High-season room in mid-range hotel €75–100 per night

Meal in mid-range taverna per person	€15–20
Taxi fare from airport to Iráklio	€5–10
Entrance fee for museums	€2–6
Car hire: small car for two weeks	€510

C

CAMPING

Crete is a popular camping destination and most sites are extremely busy in July and August. There are 17 official camp sites. Unofficial camping is prohibited. Reservations are recommended, especially in high season. The EOT has booklets listing all official camp sites and their facilities. See TOURIST INFORMATION for details.

May we camp here?	**Boroúme na kataskinósoume edó?**
We have a tent	**Éhoume mía skiní**

CAR HIRE (RENTAL)

Although Crete is well served by tour buses, it is worth hiring a car to take you off the beaten track and to free you from the tour itinerary. Cars can be hired for the day, but you get a better rate for longer periods, with either limited or unlimited mileage. Bear in mind that, because of the twisting mountain roads, most journeys are longer than they appear on the map. If you are unsure of distances, opt for unlimited mileage.

Reserving before you arrive through an international hire company will guarantee your vehicle, which can be useful, as in peak season demand will be high. **Hertz** (tel: 28103 41734; <www.hertz.com>) and **Avis** (tel: 28102 21315; <www.avis.com>) have offices at the airport, but these are not open out of office hours.

Local companies are more flexible on price, particularly in low season. **Holiday Autos** has several offices at resorts across the island. Head office: Odós 25 Avgoústou 38, Iráklio; tel: 28102 89497.

You will need a credit card for the deposit and a full national licence (held for at least one year) from your country of residence. Depending on the model and the hire company, the minimum age for hiring a car varies from 21 to 25. Third-party liability insurance (CDW) is usually included in the stated rate, and it is always worth paying a little more for comprehensive coverage.

| I'd like to hire a car (tomorrow) | **Tha íthela na nikiáso éna avtokínito (ávrio)** |

CLIMATE

Crete has an average of 320 sunny days per year. Winters are mild, although it can suddenly become cold for short spells. In general, the south coast is hotter and drier than the north. About 70 percent of the annual rainfall comes between November and February. These are the approximate monthly average temperatures in Iráklio:

		J	F	M	A	M	J	J	A	S	O	N	D
Air (max)	°C	16	16	18	21	24	28	30	39	28	26	21	19
	°F	60	60	64	70	76	82	86	86	82	78	70	66
Air (min)	°C	9	9	10	12	16	18	20	22	20	17	14	11
	°F	48	48	50	54	60	64	68	72	68	62	57	52
Sea	°C	16	16	17	18	20	23	24	25	24	23	19	17
	°F	61	61	63	64	68	73	75	77	75	73	66	63

CLOTHING

For the beach in summer, all you need is swimwear, a pair of plastic sandals and a layer to cover up to avoid sunburn. For sightseeing, shorts or lightweight trousers and T-shirts are acceptable for both sexes, or lightweight dresses for women, along with comfortable shoes for visiting archaeological sites. Dress appropriately when visiting churches or monasteries. Men should wear trousers and women a skirt that covers the knees. Both sexes should cover their shoulders. For evenings, very few places have any dress code, though smarter hotels require men to wear long trousers in the evenings.

Travelling in the mountains demands more careful planning, especially in winter and early or late in the tourist season. It is cooler than at the coast, and sudden changes in weather require that you take an extra layer of clothing whatever time of year you travel. In spring and autumn waterproof clothing is a good idea.

COMPLAINTS

Any complaints should be taken up with the establishment concerned. If this is not resolved then consult the EOT or the Tourist Police (tel: 171). These are officers specially trained to help tourists. They speak English and will advise you on further action.

CRIME AND SAFETY (See also EMERGENCIES)

Crete is a relatively safe island to visit, with very little major crime. However, as with most popular tourist destinations, petty crime such as theft from baggage and cars is on the increase so take sensible precautions: leave valuables in the hotel safe, don't carry large amounts of cash or flash around expensive jewellery and cameras; don't leave anything visible in your hire car; leave it locked with the windows/sunroof closed.

It is wise to keep separate copies of numbers of all important documents – passport, driving licence, travel tickets, travellers cheques etc – in the event of your needing replacements.

If you are a victim of crime, contact the Tourist Police (tel: 171). They have English-speaking officers who will be able to help you.

CUSTOMS AND ENTRY REQUIREMENTS

European Union (EU) citizens may enter Greece for an unlimited length of time. British citizens must have a valid passport. Citizens of Ireland can enter with a valid identity card or passport. Citizens of the US, Canada, Australia and New Zealand can stay for up to three months on production of a valid passport (South African citizens up to two months ditto). No visas are needed.

There are no limits on the amount of euros visitors can import or export, and no restrictions on travellers cheques, although cash sums of over $10,000 or its equivalent should be declared on entry.

Since the abolition of duty-free allowances for all EU countries, all goods brought into Greece from within the EU must have duty paid on them. There are no limitations on the amount of duty-paid goods that can be brought into the country.

If you are travelling from a non-EU country, allowances for duty-free goods brought into Greece are as follows: 200 cigarettes or 50 cigars or 250g of tobacco; 1 litre of spirits or 4 litres of wine; 250ml of cologne or 50ml of perfume.

Non-EU residents can claim back Value Added Tax (currently between 6 and 18 percent) on items costing over €120, provided they export the item within 90 days of purchase. Tax-free forms are available at tourist shops and department stores. Keep the receipt and form. Make your claim at the customs area of the airport when departing.

D

DRIVING

Road conditions: Crete's roads have improved greatly in the last few years, and few parts of the island are now inaccessible to a normal hire car. However, the majority of roads have no shoulders, only dust and stones at the sides, which can cause problems if you need to slow and leave the highway. Roads in the interior may be steep, with hairpin turns. Fellow road users include donkey traffic and herds of goats and sheep.

Rules and regulations: Greece drives on the right and passes on the left, usually yielding to vehicles from the right. Cretan drivers operate by their own rules, often pulling over with no warning to talk to friends, or driving on the wrong side of the road. Many island towns have one-way systems to ease the flow of traffic around the narrow streets, but many moped riders (and some car drivers) do not obey these rules. Always expect the unexpected.

Speed limits: 100 kph (65 mph) on open roads and 50 kph (30 mph) in towns, although many local people and visitors do not adhere to the regulations. Both speed-limit and distance signs are in kilometres. Seat belts are compulsory, as are crash helmets when riding a motorbike, but both are rarely used by Greek drivers. Drink-driving laws are strict and road patrols can test you and issue on-the-spot fines.

Road signs: These are mostly international and easily understood, although one problem in navigating can be a lack of names in Roman script under the Greek lettering on signposts (and you may also find the same village name spelled several different ways).

Detour	ΠΑΡΑΚΑΨΗ/**Parákapsi**
Parking	ΠΑΡΚΙΓΚ/**Párking**
No parking	...ΑΠΑΓΟΡΕΥΕΤΑΙ/...**apagorévete**
Be careful	ΠΡΟΣΟΧΗ/**Prosohí**
Stop	ΣΤΑΜΑΤΑ/**Stamáta**
Pedestrians	ΓΙΑ ΠΕΖΟΥΣ/**Gia pezoús**
Danger	ΚΙΝΔΙΝΟΣ/**Kíndinos**
No entry	ΑΠΑΓΟΡΕΥΕΤΑΙ Η ΕΙΣΟΔΟΣ/ **Apagorévete i ísodos**

Fuel costs: Cheap by European standards – petrol at around €0.80 per litre, diesel around €0.65. Petrol stations have been growing in number in recent years, but it is wise not to let your tank get too low, especially if you intend to explore the south of the island.

Parking: Although local drivers seem to park where they choose, there are enforced rules. Street parking is permissible, unless stated, but finding a space in town may be a problem. Most larger settlements have a parking area where you can leave your car at no cost; usually the village square, unless it happens to be market day.

If you need help: Always carry the telephone number of your car-hire office when you travel, as they will be able to advise you if you have difficulties. In the event of accident or theft, contact the Tourist Police who will send an English-speaking officer to help you. The Greek motoring organisation ELPA has reciprocal agreements with equivalents such as the British AA and RAC, and, if you are a member of these organisations, ELPA will provide free emergency road services (tel: 104). For non-members, ELPA's services are reasonably priced.

Are we on the right road for...?	**Ímaste sto sostó drómo gia...?**
Fill the tank please, with (lead-free) petrol	**Parakaló, geméste i dexamení (me amólivdi)**
My car has broken down	**To avtokínito mou éhi ragisméni**
There's been an accident	**Ínai distíhime**

E

ELECTRICITY

The current in Greece is 220v/50Hz. Plugs are of the European two/three-prong type. Adapters are available from electrical stores but buy at home to be sure. American and Canadian visitors will need a transformer to use their electrical appliances.

a transformer	**énas metaskhimatistís**
an adapter	**énas prosarmostís**

EMBASSIES AND CONSULATES

Australian Embassy and Consulate 37 D Soútsou Street, 115 21 Athens; tel: 21064 50404; fax 21064 66595.
British Consul Odós Papalexándrou 16, Iráklio; tel: 28102 24012.

British Embassy and Consulate 1 Ploútarchou Street, 106 75 Athens; tel: 21072 36211; fax: 21072 41872.

Canadian Embassy 4 Gennadíou Street, 115–21 Athens; tel: 21072 73400; fax: 21072 73460.

Irish Embassy 7 Vas. Konstantínou Avenue, 106 74 Athens; tel: 21072 32771; fax: 21072 40217.

South African Embassy and Consulate 60 Kifisias Avenue, 151 25 Marousi, Athens; tel: 21068 06645; fax: 21068 06640.

US Embassy and Consulate 91 Vas. Sophias Avenue, 115 27 Athens; tel: 21072 12951; fax: 21064 56282.

EMERGENCIES

Important telephone numbers:

Police/Emergency	100
Ambulance	166
Fire	199
Tourist Police	171

Fire!	**Fotiá!**
Help!	**Voíthia!**
Police!	**Astynomía!**

G

GAY AND LESBIAN TRAVELLERS

Although Crete has no specific gay scene, attitudes in the resorts are generally relaxed. Discretion is appreciated in the rural communities, which tend to have a conservative outlook on life. Homosexuality is legal in Greece for people aged over 17 years old.

GETTING THERE

By Air: Olympic Airways (<www.olympic-airways.gr>) has scheduled flights to Iráklio at least four times a day from Athens as well as fewer daily flights to Haniá and Sitiá. These can be filled quickly in summer, so book well in advance.

Aegean Airlines (tel: 28103 44324) is a private company with routes between Thessaloníki or Athens and Iráklio and Haniá.

Many visitors to Crete arrive on charter aircraft. A number of British tour operators offer flight-only and package deals from many airports in the UK; German, French, Italian and Swiss companies also fly in from around Europe.

By Boat: Crete is connected to Athens (Piraeus) by daily car and passenger ferry via Iráklio, Haniá, Réthymno and Ágios Nikólaos. Sailing time is between 12 and 20 hours. Ferries can be very busy at peak times and it is advisable to buy a ticket as far in advance as possible. The major ferry companies are Minoan (Odós 25 Avgoústou 78, Iráklio; tel: 28102 29641), Blue Star Ferries (Platía 1826, Haniá; tel: 28210 75444; <www.bluestarferries.com>) and ANEK (Odós 25 Avgoústou 33; tel: 28102 22481; fax 28103 46379; <www.anek.gr>).

GUIDES AND TOURS

You can hire a personal guide to accompany you around Knossos. They must be official guides licensed by the EOT *(see page 130)*. You will find them at the entrance to the site beyond the ticket office. For guides to accompany you to other areas, the EOT will be able to provide you with details. They can be hired by the hour or the day.

Many tour companies offer day trips by coach to the archaeological sites, Samariá Gorge and towns of Crete from wherever you are staying on the island. In the west, Diktynna Travel acts as tour agent for individual travellers. They can be contacted at Odós Agíou Márkou 6, Haniá; tel: 28210 41458; fax 28210 43930; email <diktynna@forthnet.gr>.

In Iráklio and the west, Skoutelis Travel is reliable. It can be found at Odós 25 Avgoústou 20 in the capital; tel: 28102 80808. Nostos Tour in Ágios Nikólaos are another reliable option at Odós Koundoúrou 30; tel: 28410 22819.

H

HEALTH AND MEDICAL CARE

There are no vaccination requirements for your trip to Crete.

Emergency treatment is given free, although this covers only immediate needs. EU residents can get further free treatment by presenting form E111 (available from the post office in your home country). It is always advisable to take out health/accident insurance to cover you for protracted treatment or repatriation.

Many medicines and prescription drugs widely available in other countries are banned in Greece. If you are taking any medication, always take enough for your holiday needs and keep it in its original packaging. If you have a basic medical need, look for a chemist, or *farmakío*, signified by a green cross, where you will be able to obtain advice. Most pharmacists will speak some English.

Spiny sea urchins cause a number of injuries each year, when people step on them while in the sea. Avoidance is the best option, so invest in plastic sandals to protect your feet. A more common nuisance is the mosquito, so always use insect repellent in the evenings.

Each major town in Crete has its own hospital with an emergency treatment room:

Iráklio: University Hospital, 5km (3 miles) south of Iráklio; tel. 28103 92111.

Ágios Nikólaos: on Odós Knosoú opposite the Archaeological Museum; tel: 28410 25221.

Réthymno: on Odós Trantilladou; tel: 28310 27814.

Haniá: on Odós Venizélou; tel: 28210 27231.

Dial 166 for 24-hour emergency ambulance dispatch.

a doctor/dentist	**énas giatrós/odontogiatrós**
hospital	**nosokomío**
an upset stomach	**varystomahiá**
sunstroke	**ilíasi**

HOLIDAYS

National holidays fall on the following dates:

1 January	New Year's Day or Protohroniá
6 January	Epiphany
25 March	Greek Independence Day
1 May	May Day
15 August	Assumption of the Virgin
28 October	National *Óchi* or 'No' Day
25 December	Christmas Day
26 December	St Stephen's Day

Moveable dates:

The first day of Lent (Clean Monday), Good Friday, Easter Monday, Ascension and Holy Monday (Whit Monday).

L

LANGUAGE

The sounds of the Greek language do not always correspond to exact equivalents in English, and the letters of the Greek alphabet do not always have a match in the Roman alphabet. This is the reason for so many different spellings of the same place name on road signs around the island – for example, the word *ágios* is often also spelled *ághios* and *áyios* in the Roman alphabet, although it is always pronounced the same. Emphasis is also an important element in pronouncing Greek. Throughout this book we have added an accent within each Greek name or word to show which syllable to stress.

Don't worry if you don't speak any Greek. You will find that most people working within the tourist industry will have a basic English vocabulary and many speak English very well. You will also find that the *Berlitz Greek Phrase Book and Dictionary* covers nearly all the situations you're likely to encounter on your travels.

The table on page 124 lists the Greek letters in their upper- and lower-case forms, followed by the Roman letters used in this book to transcribe them, and a pronunciation guide.

A	α	a	as in *father*
B	β	v	as in *veto*
Γ	γ	g	as in *go* (except before *i* and *e* sounds, when it's like the *y* in *yes*)
Δ	δ	d	sounds like **th** in *then*
E	ε	e	as in *get*
Z	ζ	z	same as in English
H	η	i	as in *ski*
Θ	θ	th	as in *thin*
I	ι	i	as in *ski*
K	κ	k	same as in English
Λ	λ	l	same as in English
M	μ	m	same as in English
N	ν	n	same as in English
Ξ	ξ	x	as in *box*
O	ο	o	as in *top*
Π	π	p	same as in English
P	ρ	r	same as in English
Σ	σ or ς	s	as in *kiss*, except like *z* before m or g sounds
T	τ	t	same as in English
Y	υ	y	as in *country*
Φ	φ	f	same as in English
X	χ	h	rough, as in Scottish *loch*
Ψ	ψ	ps	as in *tipsy*
Ω	ω	o	as in *long*
AI	αι	e	as in *hay*
AY	αυ	av	as in *have*
EI	ει	i	as in *ski*
EY	ευ	ev	as in *ever*
OI	οι	i	as in *ski*
OY	ου	ou	as in *recoup*
ΓΓ	γγ	ng	as in *longer*
ΓΚ	γκ	g	as in *log*
ΓΞ	γξ	nx	as in *anxious*
ΜΠ	μπ	b	as in *beg*
NT	ντ	d or nd	as in *dog* or *under*

M

MAPS

The best maps of Crete are produced by Road Editions, available from bookshops, some tourist shops and from Road Editions at 29 Odós Hándakos in Iráklio; tel: 28103 44610.

MEDIA

Television and Radio: Most large hotels have satellite TV services, which include news channels such as CNN and BBC World. On Greek stations American and English films and other imported programmes are run with Greek subtitles.

Newspapers: Most major English newspapers can be bought in resorts one day after publication. Some English tabloids are printed in Greece and are available the same day, minus the local advertisements. The *International Herald Tribune* is also available, as is the English-language *Athens News,* published daily in the capital.

MONEY

Currency: The euro (€) is the currency used in Greece. Notes are denominated in 5, 10, 20, 50, 100 and 200 euros; coins in 1 and 2 euros and 1, 2, 5, 10, 20 and 50 cents, known as *lépti* in Greece.

Currency exchange: Most banks exchange foreign currency and travellers cheques and charge a commission (usually 1–3 percent) for the service. Exchange rates should be published on a notice in the window or inside, and are generally the same for each bank.

You can also change money and travellers cheques at bureaux de change, found in all tourist centres. These often open longer hours than banks. Some advertise commission-free transactions, but exchange rates do vary, so shop around for the best deal.

You will often need to prove your identity when exchanging money, so take your passport with you.

Cash machines (ATMS): There are ATMs in the major resort areas of Iráklio, Réthymno, Haniá and Ágios Nikólaos, and in the larger settlements such as Sitiá and Ierápetra. These usually accept both major credit and debit cards. This system is generally reliable and provides the most convenient (and cheapest) way of obtaining euros.

Electric currency exchange: Next to an ATM you may also find a currency-exchange machine, which will accept notes of all major currencies outside the euro zone and deliver euros in exchange. Just follow the instructions (in English and other languages).

Credit cards: Many hotels, restaurants, ticket offices and shops accept credit cards, but there is still a sizeable minority that do not, and out in the countryside credit cards are not generally accepted. Some companies may charge extra for credit card purchases. It is always advisable to ask about credit card acceptance before you sign the register or order your food, to avoid difficulties later. It may also help to carry cash to cover meals, rather than rely on your credit card, perhaps €25–35 per person per day.

Travellers cheques: These can be used to obtain cash at banks and hotels but are not generally accepted as payment in shops, bars and restaurants.

I want to change some pounds/dollars travellers cheques	**Thélo na alláxo merikés líres/meriká dollária taxidiotikés epitagés**
Can I pay with this credit card?	**Boró na plíroso me aftí tin pistotikí kárta?**

OPENING HOURS

Opening hours vary between official organisations and privately owned shops and cafés, and also between high and low season. Always remember that the siesta is an important part of the day, and most establishments will be closed in the afternoons. If you need to get anything done it is best to visit any establishment in the morning.

Banks are open Mon–Thurs 8am–2pm, Fri 8am–1.30pm. Most museums are open Mon–Fri 8am–2pm and 5–7pm (this will vary). Most archaeological sites are open daily with no break for a siesta. Monday presents difficulties – most government sites used to be closed all day but many now open daily throughout the year; some, however, open only for a half-day on Monday, and some still close. Winter closing hours are earlier at outlying sites as they are not floodlit.

Shops are open Mon–Sat 8am–2pm and 5–8.30pm, although in peak season they may stay open throughout the day until midnight, especially when selling tourist-related products. Post offices are open 7.30am–2pm on weekdays (main post offices 7.30am–7.30pm). Stamps can also be bought from souvenir shops, newsagents and kiosks. Restaurants and tavernas begin dinner service at around 6pm, but most Greek families don't eat until after 9pm.

P

POLICE

Regular police officers wear blue uniforms. Tourist police also wear blue uniforms displaying a small national flag indicating which language they speak other than Greek. Telephone 171 in an emergency. Main police stations are located at the following addresses.

Iráklio: Odós Dikeosínis 10; tel: 28102 83190.
Ágios Nikólaos: Odós Erithroú Stavroú 47; tel: 28410 26900.
Réthymno: Odós Elevtheríou Venizélou 20; tel: 28310 28156.
Haniá: Leofóros Iráklio 23; tel: 28210 73333.

Where's the nearest police station?	**Pou íne to kondinótero astynomikó tmíma?**

POST OFFICES

Post offices are painted bright yellow with the initials ELTA and POST in English with a stylised bugle logo, and are generally open

7.30am–2pm. Stamps can be bought here, and at kiosks and tobacconists/newsagents for a small premium. Packages for non-EU countries should not be sealed until they have been checked by post office staff. Post offices also handle currency exchange, cheque cashing and money orders.

Mail boxes are also yellow with the bugle logo, but in country areas they are not emptied every day. Most hotels will post letters and postcards for you. Allow 7–10 days for postcards to Europe, 14 days for the rest of the world.

A stamp for this letter/ postcard	**Éna grammatósimo giaftó to grámma/giaftí tin kart postál**

PUBLIC TRANSPORT

Buses: There is a good network of bus services on the island, with stops at all the major archaeological sites. Journey times are long, because the buses link all the rural towns and villages along the route, but they are an excellent, cheap travel option if time is not a problem. Always arrive slightly ahead of the departure time on the timetable in case the bus leaves a little early. Tickets are bought on the bus or in advance.

Iráklio has three main bus stations, one outside the ferry port, operating services to the east of the island, one beyond the Haniá Gate in the west wall with services to the west, and a third in Platía Kýprou beyond the southern city walls, with services to the south. For information, tel: 28102 21765; <www.ktel.org>.

Réthymno bus station is on Odós Moatsou; Haniá's is on Odós Kidonias and Ágios Nikólaos at Odós Sofokli Venizélou.

Taxis: Taxis are numerous, and fares are government-controlled. They should have meters that work and are set upon departure. Taxis also make a good option for group sightseeing. Agree on an hourly or daily rate before you set off.

Boats: All the ports have ferry services that link nearby towns in addition to numerous excursion boats that run during the tourist season (some south-coast settlements are not well connected by road). The main towns for taking boat trips are: Agía Galíni, Hóra Sfakíon, Soúgia and Paleóhora. You can also hire a small boat for sightseeing excursions – ask around at the local harbour for details.

What's the fare to… ?	**Póso éhi éna isitírio giá…?**
When's the next bus to… ?	**Póte févgi to epómeno**
	leoforío giá…?

R

RELIGION

The population is almost 100 percent Greek Orthodox. However, there are Roman Catholic churches that hold regular masses at Iráklio, Ágios Nikólaos, Haniá and Réthymno.

T

TELEPHONES

The Telecommunications Company of Greece, or OTE (known to everyone as oh-tay), controls domestic and international communications in Greece. Most public telephones now accept cards for both international and domestic calls. Buy cards at OTE offices in 100-unit, 500-unit and 10,000-unit values. Kiosks and newsagents also sell the smaller unit cards. You can also make calls at street kiosks and pay after you have finished your call.

Most hotels of C class and above have direct-dial lines, but add a huge surcharge to the cost of your call. Avoid this by using an international phone card with an access number.

The international code for Greece is 30. Within Greece, wherever you are you must dial the area code – so dial 2810 for an Iráklio number, even if you are in Iráklio, for example.

TIME DIFFERENCES

Greece is two hours ahead of Greenwich Mean Time and also operates summertime, moving the clocks one hour forward between late March and late October.

In August, here is the time in the following cities:

New York	London	Dublin	Jo'burg	**Crete**	Sydney	Auckland
5am	10am	10am	11am	**noon**	7pm	9pm

TIPPING

Service is included in restaurant and bar bills, although it is customary to leave any small change on the table. If a young boy or girl brings you water or clears your table, it is customary to give them a few coins.

Taxi drivers expect a 10 percent tip. Hotel chambermaids should be left a tip of around €1 per day. Bellhops and doormen should be tipped up to €2, depending on services provided. Attendants in toilets should be left around €0.30.

TOILETS

Large towns will have public toilets, usually near the marketplace or bus station. Most museums have good public facilities.

Plumbing and sewage pipes in Greece are narrower than in other European countries and are easily clogged. Never put toilet paper into the toilet – always use the waste bin provided.

TOURIST INFORMATION

The Greek National Tourist Organisation, or Ellinikós Organismós Tourismoú (EOT), is responsible for producing and dispersing tourist information. They have a network of offices throughout the world, but official representation on the islands, including on Crete, is particularly scant. This leaves the market open to lots of unofficial information bureaux, which vary greatly in quality. For information before you travel to Greece, contact one of the following offices.

Australia and New Zealand: 51–75 Pitt Street, Sydney, NSW; postal address: PO Box R203 Royal Exchange, NSW 2000; tel: (2) 9241 16635; fax: (2) 9235 2174.

Canada: 1300 Bay Street, Main Level, Toronto, Ontario M5R 3K8; tel: (416) 9682220; fax: (416) 9686533; also 1170 Place du Frere Andre, Suite 300, Montreal, Quebec H3B 3C6; tel: (514) 8711535; fax: (514) 8711498; email <gnto.tor@sympatico.ca>.

UK and Ireland: 4 Conduit Street, London W1R 0DJ; tel: (020) 7495 9300; fax: (020) 7287 1369; email <eot-greektouristoffice@btinternet.com>.

US: Olympic Tower, 645 Fifth Avenue, New York, NY 10022; tel: (212) 421 5777; fax: (212) 826 6940; email <gnto@greektourism.com>.

For local tourist information, official EOT offices can be found at the following addresses:

Ágios Nikólaos: Akti Koundourou (opposite the little bridge across the entrance to Lake Voulismeni); tel: 28410 22357.

Haniá: 16–18 Platía 1866; tel: 28210 36155.

Réthymno: Elevtheríou Venizélou 20; tel: 28310 29148.

W

WEIGHTS AND MEASURES

Crete and Greece operate on the metric system for both.

Y

YOUTH HOSTELS

There is a handful of youth hostels in Crete. For information contact the national youth hostel organisation in your own country, or the Greek Youth Hostel Association, Odós Dragatsaníou 4, 10559 Athens; tel: 21032 34107.

Recommended Hotels

Hotels in Greece are rated by the Greek Tourist Organisation (OTE), according to the facilities available. The highest is De Luxe, moving down the scale to Luxe, A, B, C, D and E. All hotels will be clean; those in C class and above will be reasonably furnished. All hotels in the higher grades must have restaurant and conference facilities, but their standards and the comfort of their rooms may not be any higher than those of a lower class hotel.

Many larger hotels have complicated pricing systems covering rooms, junior suites/suites, the location in the hotel (water view or garden view), and whether you want to stay in low, middle or high season. High season runs from the end of July to mid-September. Prices vary greatly between high and low season in all classes of hotel. The price per night may also be less if you book for three nights or longer. Some hotels have a three-night minimum stay in high season. Always be specific when making enquiries to elicit the correct price for the time of your visit.

The following selection covers hotels and pensions (similar to hotels but simpler in style with no extra amenities) in and around the major resort areas along the north coast. From here you can head out to explore the island either independently or with an organised tour.

To make a telephone enquiry or reservation, the numbers below include the area code. The international code from outside Greece is 00 30. When calling from within Greece, even within the same town, you must dial the area code.

Prices are for a double room per night in high season.

€€€€€	over 130 euros
€€€€	100–130 euros
€€€	75–100 euros
€€	45–75 euros
€	45 euros and under

IRÁKLIO AND CENTRAL CRETE

The Atlantis Hotel €€€–€€€€ *Odós Ygias 2, 71202 Iráklio; tel: 2810 229 103; fax: 2810 226 256; email: <atlantis@atl. grecotel.gr>.* The Atlantis (part of the Grecotel chain) is especially popular with business visitors to Iráklio, but this shouldn't deter tourists from taking advantage of its efficient service and good location. Ask for a room overlooking the port. Rooms have air-conditioning, TV, phone, mini-bar, hairdryer, 24-hour room service. Facilities include restaurant, bar, pool, fitness centre, sauna, massage, roof garden, tennis, children's playground across the street. Open all year. 158 rooms.

Capsis Beach and Sofitel Palace €€€€€ *Agía Pelágia, 71500 Iráklio; tel: 2810 811 112; fax: 2810 811 076.* Occupying a large site on the Agía Pelágia Peninsula and just 22km (13 miles) from Iráklio, this is the largest complex on the island, with deluxe accommodation and facilities. The hotel also plays host to large conventions and has everything you would expect from a hotel in its class. Gardens feature a waterfall and animal park. Rooms have air-conditioning, satellite TV, phone, mini-bar, hairdryer, 24-hour room service. Facilities include private beach, indoor and outdoor pools, restaurant, bars, fitness centre, sauna/massage, tennis, kids' club, horse riding, watersports. Open all year. 495 standard rooms and bungalows.

Galaxy Hotel €€€€ *Leoforos Demokratias 67, 71306 Iráklio; tel: 2810 238 812; fax: 2810 211 211; <www.compulink.gr/galaxy>.* The finest hotel in the capital, on the Knossos road, with nicely furnished rooms and grand public spaces. Rooms have air-conditioning, TV, phone, mini-bar, room service. Interior-facing rooms are quieter, and you lose nothing as regards the view. Facilities include an indoor pool (the largest in Iráklio), sauna, bar, restaurant, pastry shop and ice-cream parlour. Open all year. 140 rooms.

Lato Hotel €€€ *Odós Epimenidou 15, 71202 Iráklio; tel: 2810 228 103; fax: 2810 240 350.* Recently renovated to a high standard, and ideal for a city stay, the Lato has many rooms with views across the harbour – ask for one of these. Within walking distance of all attractions yet reasonably quiet at night. Rooms have air-conditioning, TV, phone. There is also a restaurant. Open all year. 58 rooms.

ÁGIOS NIKÓLAOS AND THE EAST

Acratos €€€ *Odós 28 Októbriou, 72100 Ágios Nikólaos; tel: 28410 22721; no fax.* Simple, clean and pleasant hotel overlooking Lake Voulisméni, so it's right in the heart of the action. Ask for a room with balcony overlooking the lake. Rooms have air-conditioning, TV, phone. Facilities include restaurant and bar. 50 rooms.

Istron Bay Hotel €€€€ *Istron, 72100 Ágios Nikólaos; tel: 28410 61303; fax: 28410 61383; email: <istron@agn.forthnet.gr>.* Set on a hillside at Istron, 15 minutes south of Ágios Nikólaos, this hotel is an excellent combination of luxury and geniality. All rooms look out over the bay and have air-conditioning, TV, phone, mini-bar, room service, hairdryer and balcony or terrace. Facilities include restaurant serving excellent natural Cretan cuisine and with an impressive Greek wine list, pool, secluded beach, bars, shop, tennis, hairdresser, massage, entertainment programme, botanical and gastronomic classes, hiking tours, watersports. Buffet breakfast with healthy selection is included in the room rate. 113 rooms. Open Mar–Sept.

Knossos Royal Village €€€€€ *70014 Hersónissos; tel: 28970 23575; fax: 28970 23150; <www.aldemar.gr>.* This large resort hotel 5km (3 miles) outside Hersónissos is truly like a village, with low-rise pastel-and-white units laid out over a large verdant lot. Rooms, bungalows and villas are available, with separate pools and restaurants for villa guests. Furnished to a high standard, rooms are fun and brightly coloured, with air-conditioning, satellite TV, phone, mini-bar, safe, hairdryer, room service and balcony or terrace. Facilities include three pools, two restaurants, bars, shops, kids' club, health centre, tennis, dining and watersports. Guests can book treatments at the Adlemar Thalasso Spa next door. 364 rooms.

Pension Perla €–€€ *Odós Salamínos 4, 72100 Ágios Nikólaos; tel: 28410 23379; no fax.* Situated on the coastal promenade just a little way north of the harbour, Pension Perla has simple, clean rooms. A good budget choice for enjoying town life and touring the surrounding area. 10 rooms. Cash only.

Porto Eloúnda de Luxe Resort €€€€€ *72053 Eloúnda; tel: 28410 41903; fax: 28410 41889; <www.eloundahotels.com>.* One of several world-renowned hotels in this small coastal resort, the Porto Eloúnda offers refined yet laid-back luxury in a traditional Cretan-style low-rise hotel. Large rooms, bungalows and villas set on a lush green lot around a rocky inlet – many rooms have private or semi-private pools. Rooms have air-conditioning, satellite TV, phone, mini-bar, hairdryer, 24-hour room service. Facilities include three restaurants, indoor and outdoor pool, nine-hole golf course, health club, tennis, diving and watersports, shops. 163 units.

St Nicolas Bay Hotel and Bungalows €€€€€ *PO Box 47, 72100 Ágios Nikólaos; tel: 28410 25041; fax: 28410 24556; <www.stnicolasbay.gr>.* Occupying a lovely location on a headland five minutes north of Ágios Nikólaos, the St Nicolas Bay is a good luxury option for both couples and families. The complex is low-rise, with lush gardens and Cretan-style individually designed rooms and suites with traditional furniture. Some bungalows have private pools. Rooms have air-conditioning, TV, phone, safe, mini-bar, hairdryer and balcony or terrace. Facilities include restaurant, taverna, two pools and children's pool, bar, games room, shops, health club, watersports centre. Buffet breakfast included in room rate. 112 rooms. Open Apr–Oct.

HANIÁ, RÉTHYMNO AND THE WEST

Anastasia Apartments €€–€€€ *Odós Theotokopoulou 21, 73100 Haniá; tel: 28210 88001; fax: 28210 46582.* Converted 15th-century house in Topanás district of Haniá up behind the Naval Museum and within strolling distance of everything in town. Suites have kitchenettes, are well furnished and suitable for up to four people. They have air-conditioning and TV. 5 suites. Open Apr–Oct. Cash only.

Casa Delfino €€€€-€€€€€ *Odós Theofanous 9, 73100 Haniá, tel: 28210 93098; fax: 28210 96500; <www.casadelfino.com>.*

This restored 17th-century mansion surrounding an elegant Italianate courtyard is one of the delights of Haniá – and one of the best small hotels in the world. The rooms are beautifully designed and furnished. Each is a different size and style – some rooms accommodate up to six people. Luxurious living with personal service. Rooms have mini-bar (three have a kitchenette), 24-hour room service; some have a Jacuzzi. Facilities include bar, TV room. Open all year. 12 rooms/4 suites.

Creta Palace €€€€–€€€€€ *5km (3 miles) east of Réthymno; 74100 Réthymno; tel: 28310 55181; fax: 28310 54085; <www. grecotel.gr>.* This large, new village-style complex on the coastline offers great facilities to both couples and families. Rooms are pleasant – spacious and surrounded by verdant gardens, and they have air-conditioning, satellite TV, phone, room service, and balcony or terrace. Facilities include indoor and outdoor pools, restaurant, Cretan coffee shop, tennis, fitness centre, sauna, massage, kids' club, watersports. Open Apr–Oct. 312 rooms.

Doma €€–€€€ *Odós Venizelou 124, 73100 Haniá; tel: 28210 51772; fax: 28210 41578.* This converted neo-Classical mansion on the Akrotíri Road was once the British Consulate. Now it's one of the gems of Crete, not stuffy or luxurious but appealing to those who want a low-key yet personal stay harking back to the genteel old days. The owner has a prized collection of hats and has filled the public areas with antiques. Rooms have air-conditioning. Facilities include laundry, bar and a dining room serving Cretan specialities for breakfast and pre-booked dinner. Open Apr–Oct. 25 units.

Hotel Fortezza €€€ *Odós Melinissou 16, 74100 Réthymno; tel: 28310 55551; fax: 28310 54073.* This hotel on the west of town, just below the walls of the Venetian fortress, is handy for the town centre and waterfront, yet away from the noise. Not all rooms have air-conditioning, phones or balconies, so specify if you want these. Facilities include interior courtyard with pool. Open all year. 54 rooms.

Nostos Hotel €€ *Zambelioú 42–46, 73100 Haniá; tel: 28210 94743; fax: 28210 94740.* Small hotel in the heart of the Evréika district on one of the major pedestrian alleys and only a couple of minutes away from the harbour. Great for enjoying the shopping and nightlife. Rooms are small and basic but clean and have air-conditioning. Some have balconies. Open Apr–Oct. 12 rooms.

Pension Thereza €–€€ *Odós Angelou 8, 73100 Haniá; tel: 28210 92798/no fax:* This is a low-priced pension that's full of character. Set on a quaint, narrow street just behind the Naval Museum *(see page 78)*, this old mansion offers clean, bright accommodation. For a special visit, try to get rooms at the front with wrought-iron balconies. Very informal–if you arrive and reception is unattended you can simply book yourself in and pay later. All rooms with small bathrooms en suite. Roof terrace for great views over the Old Town. Open Apr–Oct. 14 rooms. Cash only.

Porto Veneziano €€€–€€€€ *Palio Limani, 73122 Haniá; tel: 28210 27100; fax: 28210 27105.* This modern high-rise hotel looks a little out of place, but its position right on the Venetian harbour in town means you only have a short stroll to be at the heart of things. Ask for a room overlooking the harbour. Rooms are comfortably furnished and have air-conditioning, TV, phone, balcony, room service. Facilities include bar. Open all year. 57 rooms.

Vamos €€ *Vamos (midway between Réthymno and Haniá); tel: 28250 23250; fax: 28250 23100.* A group of restored village houses with lovely gardens and courtyards; only a short walk from Vamos village (taverna, general store etc) and 20 minutes away from the sea. The charming buildings are simply furnished; some have fireplaces and kitchens. Rural ambience. Open all year. 8 houses.

Villa Kynthia €€€€€ *Panormós Village (postal address A&K Miliaraki SA, Dodekanissou 17, Iráklio 71306); tel: 28340 51102 or 2810 226036; fax: 28340 51148.* A beautifully refurbished 19th-century mansion in this coastal village 22km (13 miles) east of Réthymno. Each room is individually furnished, and there is a pretty courtyard and small pool. Rooms, which vary in size, have air-conditioning, telephone, refrigerator, safe and hairdryer. Facilities include a bar. Open Mar–Nov; call ahead for winter reservations.

Recommended Restaurants

Crete has no shortage of good-value tavernas around the island, although in the main resorts it may be difficult to discern those serving the best and most authentic food. If possible, follow the local people and you should find good value and delicious food. Eateries stay open late, and Greeks do not normally eat until after 9pm – don't forget that children and many adults will have taken a siesta in the afternoon. If you want the authentic atmosphere, do try to match your eating times with theirs.

Meals are generally relaxed and informal, with plenty of time for conversation. Smoking is an almost-universal habit in Greece, and closed dining areas may seem particularly unpleasant to non-smokers. Luckily, the majority of restaurants have gardens or terraces, where diners can sit out in the fresh air.

The following recommendations cover the whole of Crete and range from authentic ouzeries to good-value tavernas, with some of the most renowned restaurants for those who want a more refined setting. If you are touring they will provide good lunch spots as well as dinner venues. Unless otherwise stated, all these restaurants accept major credit cards. Most restaurants do not operate a reservation system.

The telephone numbers given include the area code, which you must dial anywhere in Greece, even if you are calling from within the area. If calling from abroad, the country code for Greece is 30.

The following prices refer to dinner per person with half a carafe (half litre) of house wine. Fish is sold by weight and will be more expensive than most other dishes.

€€€€€	more than 26 euros
€€€€	20–26 euros
€€€	15–20 euros
€€	9–15 euros
€	under 9 euros

IRÁKLIO AND CENTRAL CRETE

Giovanni's €€€ *Odós Korai 12, Iráklio; tel: 28102 46338*. Popular, established restaurant serving upmarket Greek dishes, steaks and fish. Good wine list. Eat in the panelled dining room or outside on ambient Korai Street. Open daily all year for lunch and dinner.

Ippokampus €–€€ *Odós Mitsotaki/Odós 25 Avgoústo, Iráklio; tel: 28102 80240*. The best traditional *ouzerí* in town, with views along the waterfront by the Venetian harbour. Excellent *mezédes* of all kinds. Open all year Mon–Fri for lunch and dinner. Cash only.

Loukoulos €€€€ *Odós Korai 5, Iráklio; tel: 28102 24435*. One of the most stylish restaurants in the city, with an elegant indoor dining room and a small plant-filled terrace. Mediterranean and fine Greek cuisine. Open all year Tues–Sat lunch and dinner.

Sammy's €€–€€€ *Plateia Elevtérios Venizélos, Iráklio; tel: 28102 83675*. Don't be put off by the hard sell as you approach Sammy's – the food is good and portions are generous, making it a good option in this touristy part of the city. The menu includes the usual Greek fare along with international dishes. Open daily 10am–10pm.

Zorba's €€–€€€ *On the beach, Mátala; tel: 28920 45741*. A family taverna established in the 1970s, Zorba's is one of a line along the beach here. Large portions, good prices and exceptionally fresh dishes make it special. Open daily Apr–Oct 8am–11pm. Cash only.

ÁGIOS NIKÓLAOS AND THE EAST

Castello €€€ *Odós Samoel, Ierápetra; tel: 28420 24424*. Judging by the number of Cretans eating here this is one of the best tavernas in town. Delicious barbecued and grilled meat prepared by the effervescent chef. Open daily all year, 11am–10pm.

Cretan Stars €€€€–€€€€€ *Odós Akti Koundourou 8, Ágios Nikólaos; tel: 28410 25517*. One of the most up-market restaurants in town, set in a 19th-century mansion on the waterfront. The Cretan and Mediterranean menu includes a range of seafood. Terrace or garden dining, and live music. Open Apr–Oct daily for lunch and dinner.

Itanos €–€€ *Plateia Iroon, Ágios Nikólaos; tel: 28410 25340*. A traditional taverna that has become popular with tourists yet hasn't altered its style. Good Cretan and Greek dishes, village wine and all very good value. Terrace and street tables in summer, indoor dining during the winter. Open daily all year 10am–midnight. Cash only.

Kavouri €€€ *Odós Arheou Theatrou, Limin Hersónissos; tel: 28970 21161*. Probably the most authentic cuisine in this very international resort. There is a good range of *mezédes* and a selection of stews. Daily specials. The small outside eating area is attractively decorated. Open nightly Apr–Oct for dinner only.

Kronio €€€ *Tzermiado, Lassíthi Plain; tel: 208440 22375*. Taverna on the crossroads of the largest settlement on Lassíthi. Family-run, with plain but delicious Cretan home cooking, it makes a great stop while touring the plateau. Open daily 11am–11pm. Cash only.

Migomis €€€€ *Odós Plastira, Ágios Nikólaos; tel: 28410 24353*. Romantic setting high above Lake Voulisméni. Elegant terrace and interior dining room. The menu is limited and Italian in style but excellent quality. Next door is the bar if you want to enjoy the view without food. Open daily Apr–Oct for lunch and dinner.

Pelagos €€€–€€€€ *Corner of Odós Koráki and Katehakí, Ágios Nikólaos; tel: 28410 25737*. One block back from the waterfront, north of the harbour, Pelagos is set in a fine period house and verdant garden. The entrance is graced by a small wooden fishing boat. Greek dishes and fresh seafood. Open nightly Apr–Oct for dinner.

Ta Petrina €€–€€€ *Ano Hersónissos (inland from the resort); tel: 28970 21976*. Lovely family-run taverna in a little street away from the village square. Delicious, simple Cretan dishes, washed down by quaffable village wine. Open all year for lunch and dinner. Cash only.

Taverna To Pevko €€ *Odós K. Paleogólou 18, Ágios Nikólaos; tel: 28410 23890.* Simple taverna on the walkway of Lake Voulisméni, To Pevko (The Pine) offers a limited range of Greek dishes and fresh fish. Open daily 11am–10pm. Cash only.

Vaccus €€€ *On the waterfront north of the church, Eloúnda; tel: 28410 41380.* Excellent fresh seasonal Cretan cuisine along with a range of seafood and plain steaks. Good local wine by the kilo (carafe) or the bottle. Pretty terrace. Open daily Apr–Oct 11am–midnight.

Zygos Taverna €€€ *On the main street, Istron; tel: 28410 61389.* A great example of a Cretan family taverna. They use ingredients from the family farm and create batches of dishes so you know that everything is fresh. It can get a little raucous during the tourist season, but Dimítris is a great host who's very proud of his business. Terrace and roof garden for summer dining. Open daily all year 11am–11pm.

HANIÁ, RÉTHYMNO AND THE WEST

Agira €€€ *On the harbourfront, Pánormos; tel: 28340 51022.* The pretty setting of this restaurant is matched by the delicious food, which includes a range of freshly caught seafood. The terrace has covers and windbreaks, making it good for late or early season dining. Open daily Apr–Nov, 10.30am–11pm (to 2am Jun–Aug). Cash only.

Avli €€€–€€€€€ *Odós Xanthoudidou 22 (at Odós Radamanthys), Réthymno; tel: 28310 26213.* A Venetian house containing probably the best restaurant in town. Attention to detail extends to the food, which is Cretan and Mediterranean. Worth paying the extra to eat here. Open Mar–Jan daily lunch and dinner, August for dinner only.

Livikon €€–€€€ *On the seafront, Hóra Sfakíon; tel: 8250 91261.* Seafood in abundance, but you'll also be invited up to have a look at what's fresh in the meat and salad line. Everything is excellent, including sweets such as *baklavás*. A great place for a leisurely lunch. Open daily Apr–Oct 11am–10pm.

Mathios €€€ *Aktí Enósseos, Haniá; tel: 28210 54291.* Housed in one of the old arsenal buildings on the harbour, Mathios is considered one of the best and least touristy eateries. Local dignitaries and celebrities enjoy its Cretan seafood dishes (sea urchin is a speciality). Open daily all year for lunch and dinner. Cash only.

O Mylos tou Kerata €€€–€€€€€ *On the main road, Plataniás; tel: 28210 68578.* Within the grounds of an old watermill, this restaurant has an established high reputation. Pretty courtyard or indoor dining. Cretan, Greek and Italian dishes. Spit-roasted meat a speciality. Open daily Mar–Nov for dinner, plus lunch Fri, Sat, Sun.

Nikterida (The Bat) €€€–€€€€ *Korakies, Akrotíri Peninsula; tel: 28210 64215.* It's worth driving or taking a taxi to this pretty restaurant, 15 minutes from Haniá. The setting is spectacular, with beautiful views across the bay at night. Traditional music three or four times a week. Open all year Mon–Sat for dinner only.

Restaurant Kamara €€€ *Odós Vernadou 24, Réthymno; tel: 28310 55352.* A pretty taverna next to the Museum of Historical and Folk Art. Chat to the Belgian owner about what's on the menu. Greek and international cuisine. Open Apr–Oct for lunch and dinner. Cash only.

Tamam €€–€€€€ *Odós Zambeliou 49, Haniá; tel: 28210 96080.* This former *hamam* (Turkish bath) built in 1645 has been converted into one of the best restaurants in town. Atmospheric decoration adds to the ambience, and the food is good – Cretan specialities with a variety of seasonal dishes. Open daily all year for lunch and dinner.

To Xani €–€€ *Odós Kondilaki 26, Haniá; tel: 28210 75795.* Well-known taverna serving great Cretan dishes and specialising in roast kid and lamb dishes. Live music. Open daily for dinner. Cash only.

Tholos €€€ *Odós Agion Deka 36, Haniá; tel: 28210 46725.* The dramatic setting in the ruins of a Byzantine mill makes Tholos romantic at night when the soft lights mellow the lime wash and sandstone on the walls. Greek and international dishes. Not good for a rainy day, as there is no cover. Open daily Apr–Oct for lunch and dinner.

INDEX